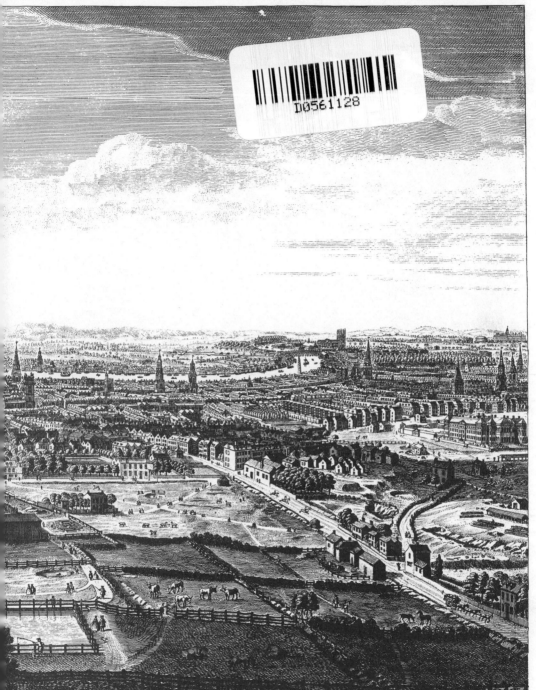

Parliament 1752.

Bowles Sculp.

Vüe de Nord de la Ville de LONDRE.

John Bowles at ÿ Black Horse in Cornhill.

Printed by PRT Offset Limited England

THE CANNING ENIGMA

Drawn from the Life by L. P. Boitard & engrav'd by him.

Elizabeth Canning.

THE CANNING ENIGMA

John Treherne

JONATHAN CAPE
THIRTY-TWO BEDFORD SQUARE
LONDON

by the same author

THE GALAPAGOS AFFAIR
THE STRANGE HISTORY OF BONNIE AND CLYDE
THE TRAP
MANGROVE CHRONICLE
DANGEROUS PRECINCTS
THE WALK TO ACORN BRIDGE

First published 1989
© John Treherne 1989
Jonathan Cape Ltd, 32 Bedford Square, London WC1B 3SG

A CIP catalogue record for this book
is available from the British Library

ISBN 0–224–02630–5

Typeset at The Spartan Press Ltd,
Lymington, Hants
Printed in Great Britain by
Mackays of Chatham PLC

for Stanley French and W-T

Author's Note

This account is based on a wealth of contemporary writings: documents, pamphlets, letters, broadsheets, cartoons, books and court proceedings. The characters are authentic, their names are real. There are about one hundred and fifty of them and – irresistibly – they speak with their own words, which I have not altered.

CONTENTS

ILLUSTRATIONS

PLATES

LINE ILLUSTRATIONS

I acknowledge the following sources of illustrations: the frontispiece and drawing on page 55, Downing College; plates 1, 3 and drawings on pages 14, 99, 104 and 138, Enfield Public Library; plates 2, 4, 6, 7, 8, 9 and 14, Guildhall Library; plates 5, 10, 11, 12, 15, 16 and drawing on page 153, British Museum Library; plate 13, courtesy of Sir Ilay Campbell; plates 17 and 18, Antiquarian and Landmark Society of Connecticut.

ACKNOWLEDGMENTS

I am indebted to the staffs of the British Library, Cambridge University Library, Cambridge City Library and the Houghton Library of Harvard University; as well as to Graham Dalling and Kate Godfrey (Enfield Public Library), Mrs S. Wickham (Dorchester Reference Library), John Crowe (Wethersfield Public Library, Connecticut), David Warrington (Harvard Law School Library) and Elizabeth Doctor (Wellcome Institute for the History of Medicine) for their expert help. Douglas Alves (Antiquarian and Landmarks Society of Connecticut), Paul Dove (Department of Prints and Drawings, British Museum), Ralph Hyde and Jeremy Smith (Department of Prints and Maps, Guildhall Library), Kate O'Donnell (Downing College Archives) and Mr S. M. Beadle (of Winchmore Hill) provided invaluable help in finding illustrations.

I am grateful to Lord Butterfield, Dorothy Frost, Austin Gresham and David Stone for advising me on medical matters, to Arthur von Mehren, Tim Briden and Paul Chipchase for legal and literary help and to Bamber Gascoigne for telling me about his family. John Overton and Francis Wei took photographs and Margaret Clements typed the manuscript with her usual skill and dedication.

The Gipsy and the Bawd

AT ABOUT NOON, a chaise rolled up bearing four women who were duly handed down and conducted through the gathering crowd. One of them, who was evidently the centre of attraction, was quite young, and desperately thin with great staring eyes; the skin of her face a darkish hue. She was carried over the threshold by the gallant who had ridden off to meet the chaise. He set her down on a long dresser against the kitchen wall. She was too tired to move or speak. Mulled wine was fetched for her from the inn. Then she was shifted to a warmer position, on a stool with her back to the open fireplace. On her right, the middle of three brace and batten doors stood open to reveal a flight of steps.

One of the men who had arrived by carriage held up his hand and raised his voice. 'Hold, gentlemen,' he called. 'This will be an Old Bailey story, and whosoever is fixed upon for committing the fact, they'll certainly be hanged. Let the room be filled full of people, and let her go and find out the people whom she accuses with robbing her. There are all the people in the parlour, she may be carried in there.'

Everyone streamed across the entrance passage into the front room.

A deaf, kindly-looking old man gave the girl some final advice. 'Bet,' he said, 'do not be daunted, for you have friends about you, and on the other hand be careful, and challenge nobody in this house without you are positive of them.'

'Sir,' the girl whispered, 'I will not.'

The gipsies were crowded together at one end of the room. The girl stood by herself at the parlour door. Mother Wells was standing on the left side of the fireplace; Mary Squires was seated in her favourite place opposite smoking her pipe. She was wearing a light-coloured cloak, her face hidden by a black bonnet and a cloth that she was holding against her cheek. Of all the prisoners, the old gipsy seemed least concerned with the turn of events.

Mother Wells decided to take the bull by the horns. She stood up and glared at the girl. 'Madam, do you know me?'

'No,' came the reply, 'I don't know that I ever saw you in my life before.'

The girl looked at George Squires without recognition. Then her eyes fell on his mother, musing away by the fire as if oblivious of all this disturbance. She raised her arm and pointed. 'It was the old woman in the corner that cut my stays off.'

There was silence in the room. Mary Squires remained where she was, gazing down into the fire.

Lucy bent forward and spoke to her mother. 'Do you hear what the gentlewoman says?' she asked. 'She said you cut off her stays.'

Again there was silence. Slowly, the old gipsy stood up, taking away the cloth to reveal her dark, swarthy face with its hideous lower lip, swollen with scrofula. 'Madam, do you say I robbed you?'

The girl gazed coolly back at the old woman. She made no reply.

'Me rob you,' the gipsy shrieked. 'I never saw you in my life before. For God Almighty's sake do not swear my life away! Pray madam, look at this face. If you have seen it before, you must have remembered it: for God Almighty, I think, never made such another.'

2

'I know you very well,' the girl replied. 'I know you too well, to my sorrow.'

And these words brought Mary Squires into the shadow of the gallows.

*   *   *

The gipsies were an odd-looking bunch. They had arrived a week before, trudging between the flat, wintry fields. Mary Squires in front pegged gamely along in a drab-coloured cloak; her dark face was made grotesque by its prodigious lower lip. Only a slight stoop betrayed her seventy years. Lucy, the younger daughter, pretty and dark-haired in a scarlet cloak, was followed by her older sister Polly: she looked tired after an illness. George, their brother, was tall and swarthy and wore a brown bob-wig; he strode along in a greatcoat with big glass-buttons, carrying a bundle under his arm.

They were heading down a frozen, rutted road towards the straggling Middlesex village of Edmonton. They had travelled a great distance from the south west, through Brentford and Tottenham. Their stock of cloth and embroidered goods was exhausted and it was a bitter January day. If they found somewhere to stay, they could rest up through the worst of the winter weather and George Squires could recover money that was owed him in London. After so many weary days on the road his old mother wanted to find a place where she could wash.

At Edmonton, they made for the house of a woman they knew who sold pease soup. But when Mary Squires said that she wanted to wash, the woman told her that it was 'not customary'. The gipsies moved on to Cheshunt. There they were directed to Enfield Wash where, it was said, they would find comfortable accommodation with a woman called Mother Wells.

So it was that the gipsy family tramped wearily at dusk beside bare ploughland. Here and there they passed dilapidated cottages and then flooded meadows. They came at last to

3

a rough and ready inn with the rising sun on its faded sign. Opposite, across the green, at the corner of Marsh Lane was a shabby, double-fronted house of brick and pantiles, with a single-storeyed wooden stable built on the side, where Mother Wells lived. Behind it there was a row of leafless black elms and, on the right, a pond ten feet away from the house.

Susannah Wells was a kindly old bawd with an unsavoury reputation. She was as likely to comfort a sick neighbour, or nip over to The Sun and Punchbowl to fetch drinks for her friends, as to procure a wench for a gentleman lodger. At Enfield Wash it was said that she had taken early to harlotry and had more than once seen the inside of Newgate Gaol. Her first husband, Mr Howit, a carpenter, had been respectable enough. He had built the workshop at the back of the house. It was now used as a loft, to prevent bargemen from the River Lea stealing the hay, as they used to when it was stored in the stable. After he died, his widow married Abraham Wells, a villainous butcher, who had been pilloried for perjury, and eventually died on the gallows.

The gipsies stayed happily enough at Mother Wells's. Mary Squires slept above the parlour in the largest bedroom, which she shared with Lucy and Polly; George had his own room at the top of the stairs, next to the one where Mrs Wells slept with her daughter and a young woman called Virtue Hall. In the hay-loft, with its crumbling lath and plaster walls, lived a farm labourer and his wife who paid ninepence a week for the privilege.

George Squires took the opportunity to straighten out his finances. He had debts in London and for this reason he was careful to keep away from his usual haunts in Newington. But two or three days after arriving at Enfield, George walked into the City to recover seven pounds fifteen shillings that he was owed.

After that they could afford soap and candles from Mr Larney's chandler's shop. They had tea and coffee – and fish could be bought from a monger who called regularly at the door. It was herring time, and herring could be cooked in

Mother Wells's kitchen, while Mary Squires smoked her pipe and warmed her old bones by the parlour fire.

The Squires family soon became a familiar sight at Enfield Wash. Mrs Howard, who lived opposite Mother Wells, let them take water from her pump; Polly curtsied to her once, she was wearing a brown stuff gown and a speckled hat. George mooched about the muddy lanes carrying a stick under his arm. It was Mary Squires who was most seen around the village, offering to mend pottery, casting a fortune for two-pence, or cadging a pipe of tobacco at a barn door.

George and his sisters loved their ugly old mother, and she loved them. In Dorset she had once walked for ten miles to look for her grown-up son when he was late back one day. She was always on the look-out for a tasty morsel for his supper – a piece of pickled pork or a black pudding – and even got up early to make buttered toast for one of his friends who had a chill. The old gipsy was proud of Lucy too, with her dark eyes and flashing white teeth. She looked so pretty in her red cloak and the white holland dress.

Life ran on without incident. Snow dusted the ground and children slid on the ice. Each morning the villagers chopped away at the pond for the horses to drink and the old gipsy pottered about or smoked in the parlour. Then on the first day of February strangers rode into Enfield Wash.

Three men came on horseback along the London road, some time after nine o'clock that morning. They dismounted at the muddy corner of Marsh Lane. There was no sign of life at Mother Wells's house, so they led their horses over to The Sun and Punchbowl and retreated to the shabby front parlour, peering out through the leaded glass with another man who had been waiting for them there. Mr Cantril, the publican, told them Mother Wells had already gone on an errand. The strangers chatted with a schoolmaster from Edmonton who called in for a drink. Then another stranger rode up, tethered his horse and walked into the parlour. He was wearing a short sword. A little later, the news went round that Mother Wells had returned.

5

They all marched out of the inn, taking the schoolmaster with them, and crossed the road, pushing open Mrs Wells's front door. Before them was a steep flight of stairs, and doors to left and right. The left-hand door was flung open, frightening Mother Wells who was entertaining some friends in the parlour.

The stranger drew his sword and cried, 'You are all prisoners.'

Leaving two men as sentries, the other four began to search the house. They cornered Mary Squires upstairs with Lucy and Polly in the best bedroom. They pushed the protesting gipsies down the stairs and into the parlour with Mrs Wells. George Squires was caught trying to escape. He had donned his hat and greatcoat and was attempting to jump from a window with a bundle of stockings under his arm when the schoolmaster took him by the collar. He too was propelled into the parlour.

'There has been a robbery,' said the man with the sword.

'When was the robbery committed?' George demanded indignantly.

'On the 1st of January.'

'We were in Dorsetshire at that time,' he replied with relief, 'at a place called Abbotsbury. We were there to keep our Christmas.'

The gipsy women shouted angrily from the parlour.

The search continued. Virtue Hall and Mrs Wells's daughter, Sal Howit, were found in their bedroom and also taken protesting down to the parlour. At the top of a short flight of stairs leading up from the kitchen to the loft a tousled woman was discovered peering down. She was Judith Natus, the labourer's wife, who had been sleeping in the loft on a pile of hay. She too was put in the parlour.

More strangers appeared. Three of them arrived hot and dishevelled on foot, and at about eleven o'clock four more came by carriage: they were a touch grander and were taken into the parlour to view the prisoners.

'How came you in this house?' one of them asked George Squires.

'I am a traveller,' he replied, 'and came here to lodge.'

'Could you not find a house of better character?'

By now there were searchers everywhere: crawling about the loft, examining a pile of human excrement on the grass below, peering at a disused jackline and pulley that communicated with the kitchen. Outside a crowd gathered – awaiting the arrival of the girl who was the cause of all the excitement.

2

The Aldermanbury Maid

ONE MONTH BEFORE, on New Year's morning, 1753, about half an hour before noon, Mary Squires's accuser had shut the door behind her and stepped out into Aldermanbury Postern – a busy warren of alleys, among the tall artisans' houses and crowded tenements clustered around one of the decaying gates in the old London Wall, just behind the Guildhall.

Elizabeth Canning was a plump eighteen-year-old, some five feet tall, with rosy cheeks pitted by smallpox, a high forehead, wide-set eyes and a long straight nose above a tight little mouth. She was in full fig, wearing a purple stuff gown, white handkerchief and apron, black quilted petticoat with a green undercoat, blue stockings and a white straw hat decorated with green ribbons. In her petticoat pocket was her Christmas wage, a golden half-guinea – in a little box given to her by her mother – three silver shillings and some coppers that she had intended as a present for her small brother had he not been saucy.

As it was New Year's Day, she had been allowed by her mistress to visit her Uncle and Aunt Colley at their house in East Smithfield, not far from Tower Hill. In the afternoon she intended to return to go shopping with her mother to buy a new

8

cloak. Elizabeth was scullery-maid to Mr Edward Lyon – a prosperous carpenter and family friend of the Cannings – who lived close by in Aldermanbury Postern and had known her since she was a small child. Her father had been a sawyer by trade and, after his death, Mrs Canning struggled to continue the business with the help of an apprentice.

Elizabeth Canning walked from Aldermanbury through the neat rows of trees in Moorfields, past the wall of Bethlehem Hospital, where the antics of the insane could always provide entertainment, along Houndsditch and into Rosemary Lane to arrive at her uncle's home at about noon. The house was immediately behind London Docks, at the eastern edge of the City, within a few minutes walk of open fields and the flat countryside running out to the villages of Bromley, Bow and Westham.

Elizabeth's Uncle Thomas was a glassblower by trade, and the Colleys lived comfortably enough in their house next to the workshop at Saltpetre Bank (now Dock Street, near Well Close Square). They kept a good table, but for dinner that day there was only cold shoulder of mutton – dressed, in preparation, the Sunday before – and potatoes. Elizabeth ate heartily, her appetite rivalling her uncle's, but her aunt was embarrassed about the cold mutton and insisted that her niece should stay for a hot supper that evening.

Mr Colley returned to his work after dinner. The shopping expedition now abandoned, Elizabeth and her aunt went into the workshop to watch him blowing and spinning away at the glowing glass. Afterwards Mrs Colley and her niece took tea together, though Elizabeth ate very little of the buttered toast.

Late that evening she was dispatched to fetch Mr Colley from The Black Boy, a tavern some seven or eight doors away, for a supper of roast sirloin of beef, washed down with some 'ten-shilling beer' which Mr Colley had in the house. Again, Elizabeth ate and drank only sparingly.

After supper, Mr and Mrs Colley walked with their niece towards the Minories, with the Tower of London on their left, hidden in the darkness, and then on to Aldgate. They parted, soon after nine o'clock, at the end of Houndsditch (a little to the east of what is now Liverpool Street station), leaving Elizabeth to make her own way back the half mile to Aldermanbury Postern. It was a surprising thing to do at that time of night; there were footpads around who regularly preyed on citizens in that part of the city.

Elizabeth Canning never returned to her master's house that night.

Edward Lyon – a kindly, slightly deaf old man – was the first to worry about her. Soon after nine o'clock, when he was ready to lock up for the night, he called on Elizabeth's widowed mother to ask if her daughter had returned from her uncle's. He came back at ten o'clock. Now thoroughly alarmed, Mrs Canning sent off her three younger children to search for their sister in Moorfields; her apprentice, James Lord, was told to walk to Saltpetre Bank to discover whether her daughter was still with the Colleys. She was frightened out of her wits when James returned with the news that Elizabeth had parted company with her uncle and aunt near The Blue Ball at the end of Houndsditch at around nine o'clock.

Mrs Canning was up before dawn the next morning and hurried over to East Smithfield, rousing Mrs Colley from her bed.

'Oh lack, has she not come in yet?' Mrs Colley exclaimed. Mr Colley was called from his workshop, but was unable to shed any light on his niece's whereabouts.

Days passed without any sign of Elizabeth Canning. Her frantic mother scoured the neighbourhood while her Uncle Thomas, with Mrs Canning's apprentice and a young woman, Mary Northam, trudged the length and breadth of the city in vain search. Prayers were said in churches and meeting houses; an advertisement was placed in the newspapers and Mrs Canning's neighbours, led by Mrs Maynard, a turner's wife, contributed their shillings to insert others. But there was no news of Elizabeth Canning, other than the report that a woman's shriek had been heard coming from a hackney coach in Bishopsgate Street on the night of 1st January.

A month later, at about a quarter to ten on the night of 29th January, just as Mrs Canning was preparing for bed in the crowded tenement house, the apprentice, James, called up to her. 'Here is somebody at the door.'

'Who is it?' asked Mrs Canning.

'Betty.'

'What Betty?'

'Our Betty!'

And Elizabeth Canning herself burst in to the room screaming, and ran to the chimney-piece. Mrs Canning shrieked 'Feel her, feel her' – apparently to make sure that her daughter was not a ghost.

The girl was in a shocking state. She was almost doubled up, holding her hands before her and, according to her mother's account, 'walking sideways'. Her face and hands were black. She was wearing only a shift, a filthy petticoat and a bedgown. A dirty rag was tied round her head, drenched with blood from a wound over her ear.

According to James Lord his mistress 'fell in a fit' when she saw her daughter and remained unconscious for some minutes. When she recovered she sent him to fetch help from the neighbours. The first to arrive was Mrs Woodward ('a broker in goods'), followed by Polly Lyon (the daughter of Elizabeth's employers). Then a Mrs Myers arrived and a servingmaid from one of the neighbours, with John Wintlebury, landlord of The Weaver's Arms and Elizabeth's former master, and Robert Scarrat, a journeyman hartshorn-scraper, who lodged next door but one to Mrs Canning in the house of a potter in Aldermanbury Postern. He had heard the excited calls of the apothecary's maid – 'Betty Canning is come home.' As the room filled up, Elizabeth Canning began to tell her story, encouraged by the kindly Wintlebury who held her hand and asked gently, 'Where have you been?'

It was an extraordinary tale.

After leaving her aunt and uncle at Houndsditch, she was attacked by two men near Bedlam Wall as she was passing through Moorfields. They stole her money, stripped off her gown and knocked her to the ground. When she recovered consciousness she found herself being dragged along a country road. At around four o'clock that morning, she was carried into a house where there was an elderly woman and two younger ones. The older woman took hold of her arm and asked if Elizabeth would 'go their way'. When she refused, the woman cut off her stays – those bastions of eighteenth-century virtue – slapped her in the face and pushed her up some stairs to a room.

The room was empty save for some lumber, a pitcher of water and some pieces of mouldy bread. In the fireplace was the bedgown and the rag that she was now wearing.

She was locked in the room for a month. During this time, no one spoke to her or came into the room or brought her any more food or water. Eventually, she summoned up courage to pull some boards away from a window, squeezed through the opening and climbed down to the ground, cutting her head in so doing.

She staggered home five hours later.

In response to a question from Mr Wintlebury, Elizabeth said that the house in which she had been imprisoned must have been on the Hertford Road, because – when peering through a crack in the boarded window – she saw a coach go by, driven by a coachman who used to drive her mistress into Hertfordshire.

It was at this point that Robert Scarrat, the journeyman hartshorn-scraper, entered the proceedings.

'I'll lay a guinea to a farthing, she has been at Mother Wells,' he said. 'For that is as noted a house as any is.'

Elizabeth Canning agreed that, during her imprisonment, she had heard the name of 'Mother Wells' or 'Wills'.

This was enough for the assembled company crowding round the exhausted scullery-maid and arrangements were set in train to get with all speed to Mother Wells's establishment. Robert Scarrat knew exactly where to go. He had lived at Edmonton and had visited Mother Wells at Enfield Wash on more than one occasion.

The first move was to apply for a warrant against Mother Wells on suspicion of robbery. Accordingly, Elizabeth and a large contingent of neighbours, with Robert Scarrat in tow, appeared before Alderman Chitty at the Guildhall two days later. About fifty of them crowded into the Justice Room. The Alderman listened carefully to Elizabeth Canning's story, interrupting only to enquire about her natural functions during her imprisonment (she said she 'had no stool at all and made only a little water') and to ask her to describe, as exactly as possible, the room in which she claimed to have been imprisoned in the house at Enfield Wash. She testified that she had been locked in a small, square room which was furnished with only a chair or two, an old table and a picture above the chimney. She had had to sleep upon the bare floor.

After considering the evidence, Alderman Chitty issued a warrant for the apprehension of Susannah Wells and her accomplices at Enfield Wash.

The following morning, Thursday, 1st February, a veritable cavalcade left Aldermanbury for Enfield Wash. Elizabeth and Mrs Canning travelled by chaise, with Mrs Myers and a Mrs Garrat – an uncomfortable enough journey over the notorious Hertford road which, in winter, was a rutted mire. Mr White, the 'Marshal's man', an officer of the Lord Mayor, rode ahead. Accompanying him, in high feather – on horseback or on foot, straggling along the Hertford road – were a dozen or more Canning friends and supporters, including Elizabeth's uncle, Thomas Colley; the publican, John Wintlebury; and Robert Scarrat, who had come in uninvited to take such a prominent part in the proceedings. Other neighbours and friends of friends came in a carriage, including Edward Lyon and his friend, Gawen Nash, owner of a coffee-house in Gutter Lane, together with *his* pal John Hague, the goldsmith, and Edward Aldridge, a silversmith.

After they had locked up the inhabitants in the parlour, White and his retinue had time to look around. They examined the three bedrooms over the parlour, and the kitchen, from which the workshop or loft could be reached through a door at the bottom of a flight of eight steps. There was also a cellar which was full of water. In the kitchen was a dresser with a drawer: Canning had alleged that a knife had been taken from just such a dresser in order to cut her stays.

Mother Wells's kitchen, showing the stairs into the loft where Elizabeth Canning said she was 'confined'

None of the bedrooms corresponded in any way with the room which Elizabeth had described in her deposition to Alderman Chitty. Only the loft, built on by Mr Howit, was anything like the one in which she had sworn she had been incarcerated. It was a long, narrow room – dilapidated, with crumbling lath and plaster walls – containing an assortment of jumble. There was also a pile of hay, stored there to prevent the bargemen from stealing it.

Canning had made no mention of hay and her companions were anxious on this point. While they were waiting, they spun a coin to see who should have the honour of riding back to meet the chaise to question Elizabeth about the hay. Joseph Adamson, a currier – and childhood friend of Elizabeth

Canning – won the toss and rode off. When he reappeared he was waving his hat.

'We are all right, for Bet says there is a little hay in the room.'

When the chaise arrived, and Elizabeth Canning had drunk her mulled wine and accused Mary Squires, she was led back into the kitchen and then up the eight stairs to the loft.

'This is the room I was in', she said immediately, 'but there is more hay in it than there was when I was here.'

The girl pushed some hay aside with her foot to reveal two holes in the floor. She said she had seen them before. When a pitcher, which was on the floor, was held up, she said: 'Yes, that is the jug I had my water in.' Canning also pointed out a tobacco mould, a basin, saddles, a cask and a pewter basin – objects which she said she had mentioned on her arrival at her mother's. When Joseph Adamson put his back against the window and asked what could be seen from it, she was able to describe the view ('some hills a pretty way off and one, two or three houses on the left-hand side'). Furthermore, the boards that shuttered the window, through which she said she escaped, had only recently been fastened there ('the wood was fresh split with driving a great nail through it, and the crack seemed as fresh as could be').

The evidence was damning. All the inmates were straightaway dragged to the house of a local magistrate, Mr Merry Tyshmaker, of Ford's Grove, Edmonton. Two were committed for trial: Mary Squires – for stealing Elizabeth Canning's stays – and Mother Wells, as accessory to the felony.

3

Mr Justice Fielding

WITHIN DAYS OF the expedition to Enfield Wash, the affairs of
the carpenter's scullery-maid embroiled one of the most
celebrated figures of his age. At forty-five – worn out as much
by quarrelling and acrimony, and the drinking and gluttony of
his time, as by incessant writing – the creator of Tom Jones and
Molly Seagrim was approaching the end of his turbulent life.

Four years before, by the influence of the Duke of Bedford,
Henry Fielding had taken the sacrament at St Paul's, Covent
Garden, to become Justice of the Peace for Middlesex and
Westminster. Although lampooned by wits and garret-scribb-
lers – as a hunter after fortunes, living on kept mistresses and
pursued by duns and bumbailiffs – Fielding threw himself with
volcanic energy against the crime and vices of Hogarth's and
Elizabeth Canning's London: 'in which a thief may harbour
with as great security as wild beasts do in the deserts of Africa
or Arabia'. Despite the sneers of Horace Walpole and Tobias
Smollett, and fortified by every kind of quack medicine, Justice
Fielding administered the law with vigour and determination
from a tall, four-storeyed house on the west side of Bow Street.
He sentenced a sailor, Bosavern Penlez, to hanging for stealing
lace bands, caps and ruffles, to the value of fifteen shillings, as

well as advocating the abolition of public executions (the 'Tyburn holiday') on the grounds that they made heroes of criminals. Fielding also recognized the urgent need for reform. In 1753 he devised an ambitious scheme by which huge workhouses should be built, each capable of housing five thousand destitute people, in which useful trades were to be taught, the sick to be tended in a hospital and the wicked taken to the whipping-post.

In December 1751, what was to be Fielding's last novel had been published. *Amelia* is the story of a beautiful, forgiving woman, ruined by a spineless ne'er-do-well of a husband; an inveterate gambler who drags her down to the depths of vice and folly that from his years as a magistrate Fielding knew only too well. There was uproar from the critics, especially about the heroine's nose. Dr Johnson opined that the 'vile broken nose . . . ruined the sale of the book'; Smollett considered Amelia no better than 'a wench who had lost her nose in the service of Venus'; for the snob Samuel 'Serious' Richardson (whose best-selling novel, *Pamela*, was a detailed record of the attempts of a man of fashion to seduce a fourteen-year-old serving maid) it was 'beyond my conception that a man of family, who had some learning, and who really is a writer, should descend so excessively low in all his pieces'.

But Henry Fielding knew, with all the insight of the writer, and experience as a magistrate, the depths of human degradation and the sometimes desperate plight of women in eighteenth-century London.

This, then, was the tired, dishevelled giant of a man, with jutting chin and Roman nose, on whom Elizabeth Canning's solicitor called just five days after the visit to Mother Wells's house at Enfield Wash.

Henry Fielding was upstairs in the drawing-room at his house in Bow Street that afternoon. Fatigued, almost literally to death, he was taking tea with his wife and longing for a few days away from the smells and smoke of London – at his farmhouse in open countryside between Ealing and Acton – when his clerk appeared carrying yet another pile of papers, this one endorsed at the top: 'The case of Elizabeth Canning, for Mr Fielding's opinion'.

Wearily, but still noting that his fee was enclosed, Fielding handed the bundle to his wife, telling George Brogden to give his compliments to Mr Salt and say that he intended taking the case with him to Fordhook. He would bring it back on the following Friday morning.

Brogden reappeared almost immediately, accompanied by Mr Salt who followed him into the room. The case would present little difficulty, the solicitor assured Fielding, but it was of the utmost urgency to make haste.

'Upon this', Fielding later recounted, 'I desired him to sit down; and when the tea was ended, I ordered my wife to fetch me back the case, which I then read over, and found it to contain a very full and clear state of the whole affair relating to the usage of this girl, with a query what methods might be proper to take to bring the offenders to justice; which query I answered in the best manner I was able.'

Mr Salt was so insistent that Henry Fielding agreed to examine Elizabeth Canning and Virtue Hall; partly because of the extraordinary nature of the case, but also for 'a great compassion for the dreadful condition of the girl, as it was represented to me by Mr Salt'.

The following morning, Elizabeth Canning was carried in a closed chair to No. 4, Bow Street, followed on foot by Mr Salt and a contingent of Aldermanbury men. Mr Wintlebury and Robert Scarrat handed her from the chair and helped her up the staircase to Henry Fielding's room above the court.

Mr Justice Fielding gazed at the skinny little maid, her eyes huge in her wasted face.

Mr Salt explained that her story had been taken and set down: it would only be necessary for him to read it. How she had gone to see her uncle and aunt at Saltpetre Bank, and that, on her return home, had been set upon by two men – both wearing brown bob-wigs and drab-coloured greatcoats – opposite Bethlehem Gate in Moorfields. One of the men struck her a violent blow on the right temple. They dragged her to the place at Enfield Wash – reputedly 'a very bad and disorderly bawdy house' – where the old gipsy woman took hold of her hand and promised to give her fine clothes if she would 'go their way', which, Canning understood meant to become a prostitute. With the gipsy were two younger women. The old woman took a knife out of a kitchen drawer, cut the lace of her stays and took them away from her. As soon as the men left, the old gipsy woman pushed her up 'an old pair of stairs' and into a back room, like a hay-loft. If she made the least noise, she was told, her throat would be cut. At dawn, she discovered a large black jug, with the neck much broken, containing some water and several pieces of bread ('near in quantity to a quartern loaf') and 'a small parcel of hay'. She was left in this room from the morning of Tuesday, 2nd January, until about half-past four in the afternoon of Monday, 29th January. No one came to her during the whole of this time, although she could hear voices and often the name of 'Mrs and Mother Wells called upon'.

By Friday, 26th January – Mr Salt told Henry Fielding – Elizabeth Canning had consumed all the bread and water and was 'almost famished with hunger and starved with cold and almost naked'. Three days later she 'broke out at a window' and walked back to London, reaching her mother's home at about quarter-past ten that night. Since then she was in a 'very weak and declining state and condition of health, and although all possible care and affluence is given to her, yet whatever small nutriment, she, this informant, is able to take, the same receives no passage through her, but what is forced by the apothecary's assistance and medicine.'

Henry Fielding was impressed by Elizabeth Canning – by her modesty and gentleness of manner – and quickly convinced of the truth of her story. With barely a second thought he added his signature to Mr Salt's document, beside the scullery-maid's laboriously-scrawled mark, and issued a warrant against all 'who should be found resident in the house of the said Wells, as idle and disorderly persons and persons of evil name'.

George, Lucy and Polly had fled from Enfield Wash, but Virtue Hall and Judith Natus were seized and taken up to Bow Street.

'They were in my house above an hour or more before I was at leisure to see them', Fielding later wrote, 'during which time, and before I had ever seen Virtue Hall, I was informed that she would confess the whole matter. When she came before me she appeared in tears, and seemed all over in a trembling condition, upon which I endeavoured to soothe and comfort her.'

'Child, you need not be under this fear and apprehension,' he told her. 'If you will tell us the whole truth of this affair, I give you my word and honour, as far as it is in my power to protect you, you shall come to no manner of harm.'

Virtue Hall dried her eyes and promised to tell the truth, pleading for time to recover from her fright. Fielding ordered a chair to be fetched for her and after several minutes – when her sobs had died – began quietly to question the frightened little whore, using his 'softest language and kindest manner'.

But not for long, for the answers were not at all to Mr Justice Fielding's liking.

'She had been guilty of so many prevarications and contradictions that I told her I would examine her no longer, but would commit her to prison and leave her to stand or fall by the evidence against her and, at the same time, advised Mr Salt to prosecute her as a felon, together with the gipsy woman.'

Fielding's bullying had the desired effect. The frightened girl begged to be heard again, promising to tell the whole truth; saying that she had not done so before for fear of the old gipsy and Mother Wells.

Once more Fielding questioned Virtue Hall. Now the answers were consistent; they agreed with Elizabeth Canning's testimony. Satisfied, Henry Fielding told the girl to go with Mr Salt who would take down her evidence in writing.

'Be a good girl,' Fielding called after her. 'And be sure to say neither more nor less than the whole truth.'

For two hours, until near midnight, Virtue Hall sat with Elizabeth Canning's solicitor before they returned together with a written account of her testimony – which now tallied with the scullery-maid's story in every important respect. Virtue Hall testified that she heard the old gipsy's son tell his mother that he brought the girl from Moorfields, after removing her gown, apron and hat and taking half a guinea. She had no idea of the identity of the other man involved. Hall further maintained that Mary Squires cut the laces of Elizabeth Canning's stays – wrenching them from her and then hanging them on the back of a chair – before pushing the captive up the stairs to the loft. She also testified that, after about two hours, water in an old broken-mouthed large black jug was carried up the stairs and put down on the floor of the loft. Fortune Natus and his wife had slept on a pile of hay in the kitchen and *not*, as they had sworn before Mr Tyshmaker, in the loft where Elizabeth Canning had been imprisoned. Mother Wells's daughter, Sarah, had afterwards nailed up the loft window through which Elizabeth Canning escaped so that it 'might not appear to be broke open'. Virtue Hall had known Mother Wells for 'about a quarter of a year' and knew – only too well – that she kept 'a very notorious ill governed and disorderly house and has the character of doing so for many years'.

After he had finished with Virtue Hall, Fielding next examined Judith Natus. She stubbornly maintained that she and her husband had slept on the bundle of hay in the loft and that she had never seen nor heard of any such person as Elizabeth Canning, before she had burst in with her friends two weeks before.

There was some indignation on the part of the onlookers while Henry Fielding was carrying out his examination and the call went up that Judith Natus should be committed for perjury. Fielding would have none of this, maintaining that he might as well commit Virtue Hall upon the evidence of Judith Natus. But he was, nevertheless, privately convinced that Judith Natus was lying and warned her to be 'very sure of the truth of what she said, if she intended to give that evidence at the Old Bailey'.

After talking again to Virtue Hall, and ordering detainers for felony against Mary Squires and Susannah Wells, Henry Fielding retired to his bed with the intention of departing for Fordhook in the morning.

When he left for Fordhook, Fielding believed he had 'ended all the trouble which I thought it necessary for me to give myself in this affair'. Yet he was mistaken, for on his return to Bow Street his clerk came to his room to tell him that several noble lords had sent to the house desiring to be present at an examination of the gipsy woman.

Fielding acted promptly, ordering Mary Squires and Susannah Wells to be brought from prison, and summoning Mr Salt, the solicitor, requesting him to bring Elizabeth Canning and Virtue Hall to the courtroom on the ground floor of his house at Bow Street. Lord Montfort, and several other gentlemen of fashion, attended on the appointed day. The assembled company listened as the charges were read to the two prisoners and while Justice Fielding asked 'a very few questions' and, after, as Elizabeth Canning and Virtue Hall recited their evidence.

Henry Fielding believed that he had now firmly settled the matter. But he was wrong, for all England would soon know of the old gipsy woman and the scullery-maid from Aldermanbury – *and* of his hand in the proceedings.

4

The Midwife's Tale

WHILE ALL THE official examinations and depositions were going on, an unofficial inquisition took place at Mrs Canning's house. The inquisitor was the formidable Mrs Mayle, the Aldermanbury midwife who had delivered Elizabeth, eighteen years before.

Elizabeth Mayle called – a few days after the expedition to Enfield Wash – to discover whether there was any news of poor Widow Canning's daughter.

The widow poured out her troubles as soon as the midwife appeared over the threshold.

'Madam, Oh Lord, Madam,' the distraught mother wailed. 'Have you heard of my misfortune?'

Mrs Mayle said that she had, indeed, read about it in all the newspapers and had called to learn if there was any news of Elizabeth.

'Yes,' replied Mrs Canning. 'She has come home as naked as she was born.'

'Oh Lord,' Mrs Mayle said. 'What, without a shift on?'

'No, she had a shift on.'

'Where is she then?'

'Behind you.'

Mrs Mayle turned and exclaimed. 'Lord, bless me! Bet, how come this about?'

Elizabeth Canning was lying on a bed. She told of the two men who had robbed her and knocked her down in Moorfields.

'My dear,' said the midwife. 'Don't trouble yourself about these things, for God Almighty will raise your friends to get you more. I hope the men did not use you ill, so as to debauch you.'

She could not tell, Elizabeth Canning said, for she had had fits.

'What did they do with you after they had robbed you?' asked Mrs Mayle.

'They carried me to Enfield Wash.'

'Where is Enfield Wash?'

'Out of town,' Elizabeth replied.

She then told of how an old gipsy woman had cut her stays, called her a bitch and had locked her in a room for a month.

The curiosity and professional instincts of the midwife were now thoroughly aroused.

'Mrs Canning,' said she. 'Have you got this shift your daughter went abroad in? Sure never was such a case before.'

Mrs Canning reached out for the shift.

'I'll tell you if anybody has debauched your child, if you'll let me see it,' the midwife said, taking the garment from the widow and peering at it expertly. 'Mrs Canning,' she said, 'is this the shift your daughter went away in?'

'Yes!'

'I suppose it was washed since she has been gone?' the midwife enquired.

'No, how could that be', replied Mrs Canning, 'for she was in a room where nobody came to see her.'

Mrs Mayle now turned her attention to the victim. 'I think the shift is too clean, except you have had it washed since you have come home.'

'No,' said Elizabeth, 'it had not been washed.'

Mrs Mayle then delivered her judgement. 'Then, my dear, you may make yourself easy, for I can see it, that no man has debauched your child; but it is uncommonly clean to be wore so long.'

The next thing to be cleared up was the matter of Elizabeth's constipation: Mrs Mayle decreed that glysters [enemas] should be administered forthwith.

As Mrs Mayle prepared to leave, Mrs Canning sent one of her children to fetch her neighbour, Mrs Woodward.

When she arrived, Mrs Canning turned to the midwife. 'Will you say what you said before?'

'Yes, Mrs Canning,' said Mrs Mayle, 'with all the pleasure in life. If this shift has not been washed, I'll make an oath before a judge no man had copulation with her.'

With that, Mrs Mayle departed. But not for long, for her curiosity was roused on another matter. Within half an hour she was back at Elizabeth Canning's bedside. 'Bet,' she said, 'I was very sorry I did not ask you whether your feet were not very sore in walking barefoot.'

'No they are not,' came the reply. 'I had my shoes and stockings on, they did not take them from me.'

The midwife concluded that it must have been Mrs Canning's agony of mind that had led her to say that her daughter had come home naked. 'What more had you on?'

'My under-petticoat and an old bedgown, which I found in the corner of the room.'

Mrs Mayle appeared satisfied. 'Good-bye, child,' she said.

As she turned to leave Mrs Canning flung herself down to kneel at the midwife's feet with her hands held up.

'Thank God, my daughter is not a whore.'

*   *   *

Two days later Mrs Mayle called again. There were visitors with the Cannings: two young women, and an older, grave-looking one who Mrs Mayle did not know, but was impressed by her appearance of gentility.

Mrs Mayle came to the point directly. 'Mrs Canning, I am come to ask if Bet has had a stool.'

25

'No,' came the reply.

'Then she must die', pronounced the midwife, 'without you have given her glysters and she has relief that way. Why did you not give it her?'

Mrs Canning said that she had.

'Did anything come off with it?'

'Yes, a little.'

'If nothing more came off, she is a dead girl, and all the world can't save her life.'

So saying, Mrs Mayle took Elizabeth's right hand in her left and pronounced more dire warnings. 'Now she seems as cold as death, and if she has no passage she must die, and all the world can't save her.'

By this time, Elizabeth's other visitors had had enough.

'How can you frighten the girl out of her life, to tell her she must die, when she has no fever?'

'Did you ever hear there was such a thing before?' came the midwife's reply. 'There is one thing in her favour, though, she has not been debauched.'

The irrepressible Mrs Mayle sailed on regardless. 'Reach the shift,' she commanded the grave woman – the one who had impressed by her gentility – and then turned to Mrs Canning. 'Let her judge the case and see that your child has not been debauched.'

The woman inspected the shift. 'I don't see anything like it.'

'Look over it well,' urged Mrs Mayle. 'Do you think this has been worn three weeks and three days?'

'No,' said the grave woman. 'I don't think it has, I don't think that is likely.'

Poor Mrs Canning was now beside herself. 'Do you come here to set my other friends against me?'

But Mrs Mayle continued relentlessly, first on the matter of three spots of excrement that she had spotted on the garment and then, on the matter of Elizabeth's menstruation ('there were no marks of her being according to the course of other women').

Mrs Canning responded that her daughter had been 'out of order' for three or four months as the result of a cold.

And there ended – for the time being – the matter of Elizabeth Canning's shift.

5

The Old Bailey

MARY SQUIRES AND Susannah Wells were brought across the Sessions Yard from Newgate prison – that 'bottomless pit of violence' – to face trial in the Old Bailey on 21st February, 1753. The court sat on the ground floor of the tall, three-storeyed Sessions House.

Despite the hazard of gaol-fever, which three years before had killed more than sixty people at the 'Black Assize', the balustraded stone galleries were packed with excited spectators; who gazed down at the two frightened old women in the bail dock, with its spiked rim to discourage more agile occupants from escaping across the Sessions Yard.

Raised up, and fenced off, at the other end of the crowded courtroom were the Lord Mayor of London, Sir Crisp Gascoyne – splendid in brocade and full-bottomed wig, his chain of office about his neck – and His Majesty's Justices of Oyer and Terminer, each with his nosegay of flowers to ward off the prison smells. Below them, the bewigged, black-gowned lawyers lounged at a long, book-laden table, their ink and quills, parchments and nosegays before them.

At fifty-two Sir Crisp Gascoyne was an influential and vigorous man; a force in the City and the first occupant of the

28

newly-built Mansion House. He had set up business as a brewer in Gravel Lane, Houndsditch, married the daughter of a wealthy physician, Dr Bamber, and had risen to be Master of the Brewers' Company, Alderman of Vintry Ward and Sheriff of London and Middlesex. Sir Crisp had been knighted, three months before, on the occasion of his presenting a loyal address to the King. A powerful man with a handsome oval face, he had shouldered public responsibilities as well as the acquisition of wealth. Four years earlier, as head of the committee of City lands, he had forced through the Common Council an act for the relief of the orphans of the City of London and was known for his good works in Essex, where he had purchased large estates.

The charge that was read before Sir Crisp, the Hon. Mr Justice Wright, the Hon. Mr Justice Gundry and the Hon. Mr Baron Adams indicted Mary Squires, widow: 'for that she, on the 2nd of January, in the dwelling house of Susannah Wells, widow, on Elizabeth Canning, spinster, did make an assault, putting her the said Elizabeth Canning in corporal fear and danger of her life, and one pair of stays, value 10 shillings, the property of the said Elizabeth, from her person, in the dwelling house, did steal, take, and carry away. And the latter, for that she well knowing her the said Mary Squires to have done and committed the felony aforesaid on the 2nd January, her the said Mary did then and there feloniously receive, harbour, comfort, conceal and maintain, against His Majesty's peace, and against the form of the statute'.

The charge was a serious one, for the value of Elizabeth Canning's stays would mean that Mary Squires would hang on the Tyburn tree if she were found guilty on the indictment.

*　　*　　*

Elizabeth Canning had been cheered into the Sessions House by the mob and the spectators in the crowded galleries, and pressing on to the floor of the court, they hung on her every word. A diminutive figure with all eyes fixed upon her, she gave a clear account of how she had spent the afternoon of the 1st January with her Uncle and Aunt Colley and that, having left her at Houndsditch to find her own way to Aldermanbury, two 'lusty men, both in greatcoats' had laid hold of her, one on each side, and taken the half guinea and the three shillings from her.

'Were there any persons walking near you at that time?' enquired Elizabeth's counsel, Mr Stow.

'I saw nobody,' came the reply. 'They then tied my hands behind me; after which one of them gave me a blow on the temple, and said, "Damn you, you bitch, we'll do for you by and by." I having been subject to convulsion-fits these four years, this blow stunned me, and threw me directly into a fit.'

Elizabeth Canning's replies came clearly and lucidly as her counsel led her through her evidence.

'Are these fits attended with struggling?'

'I don't know that.'

'What happened afterwards?'

'The first thing that I remember after this was, I found myself by a large road, where was water, with the two men that robbed me.'

'Had you any discourse with them?'

'I had none; they took me to the prisoner Wells's house.'

'About what time do you think it might be?'

'As near as I can think, it was about four o'clock in the morning. I had recovered from my fit about half an hour before I came to the house. They lugged me along, and said "You bitch why don't you walk faster?" One had hold of my right arm, the other on my left, and so pulled me along.'

Canning then related how the two men dragged her along by her petticoats and that she arrived at Mother Wells's house at about three hours before daylight.

'When you was carried in, what did you see there?'

'I saw the gipsy woman Squires, who was sitting in a chair, and the two young women in the same room; Virtue Hall was one; they were standing against the dresser.'

The counsel pointed towards Susannah Wells. 'Did you see the prisoner there?'

'No, I did not. As soon as I was brought in Mary Squires took me by the hand, and asked me if I chose to go their way, saying, if I did, I should have fine clothes. I said, "No."'

'Did she explain what she meant by going their way?'

'No, Sir. Then she went and took a knife out of a dresser-drawer and cut the lace of my stays, and took them from me.'

'Had you, at that time, any apprehensions of danger?'

'I thought she was going to cut my throat, when I saw her take the knife.'

Mr Stow again pointed to Susannah Wells. 'Did you see the prisoner at the time?'

'No, I did not.'

'Was there anything else taken from you?'

'There was not; but Squires looked at my petticoat, and said, "Here you bitch, you may keep that, or I'll give you that, it is not worth much", and gave me a slap on the face.'

The old gipsy woman had pushed her up the stairs from the kitchen – there were four or five of them – and shut her in a place 'they called the hay-loft'. When daylight came, she saw that the room contained a fireplace, with a grate in it, and nothing but hay to lie upon. There was a black pitcher 'not quite full of water' and about twenty-four pieces of bread (making 'about a quarter loaf' in all). Canning also mentioned that she had a penny mince-pie in her pocket that she had bought the previous day to take home for her brother.

'How long did you continue in that room?' counsel asked.

'A month by the weeks, all but a few hours.'

'What do you mean by a month by the weeks?'

'I mean a four-weeks month.'

Carefully, Elizabeth Canning's counsel guided her through her evidence. She answered with assurance, and just the right degree of deference, telling how she broke through the boarded window and jumped down on to soft, clayey ground, cutting her ear as she did so, and followed the road towards London and, eventually, to Aldermanbury Postern.

Elizabeth Canning was cross-examined by Mary Squires's counsel. William Davy was a Devon man – ex-grocer, former debtor – now the up-and-coming criminal defence lawyer of his time. Quick and intelligent, with a dry, sardonic wit, he commenced, innocently enough, by asking about the attack in Moorfields and Elizabeth Canning's arrival at Mrs Wells's house. Then came a succession of rapid thrusts.

'Was you in any surprise when she took your stays?'

'I was in great surprise – and all of a tremble.'

'Then how can you tell who was there at the time?'

'The terror made me look about me to see what company was there.'

'How long did the two men stay in the room?'

'They stayed no longer than till they saw my stays cut off, then they went away, before I was put up in the loft.'

'Did you not make an attempt to get out before that Monday you talk on?'

'I did not,' came the swift response.

'How come you not to make an attempt before?'

'Because I thought they might let me out; it never came into my head till that morning.'

Elizabeth Canning answered every question directly and with complete composure.

'Had you any of your fits while in that room?'

'I had not, but was fainting and sick.'

At this point, Mary Squires, who had been grumbling away to herself in the dock, could bear it no longer. 'I never saw that witness in my lifetime till this day three weeks,' she bawled.

William Davy used the interruption to turn his questioning towards the old gipsy.

'How was the prisoner dressed when you was carried in?'

'She was sitting in her gown, with a handkerchief about her head.'

Another pat answer from the Aldermanbury scullery-maid: William Davy could not shake her.

The next witness was Virtue Hall. Mr Stow led her through her evidence – which tallied on almost every point with Elizabeth Canning's – while Mary Squires fulminated in the dock. She eventually burst out as Virtue Hall was telling how she was forced to do as she was told at Mother Wells's house.

'What day was it that the young woman was robbed?' the old gipsy broke in.

'She says on the morning of the 2nd January,' counsel replied.

'I return thanks for telling me, for I am as innocent as the child unborn,' Mary Squires retorted.

Then Mother Wells joined in.

'How long were these people [the gipsies] at my house in all, from first to last?'

'They were there six or seven weeks in all,' Virtue Hall replied, 'they had been there about a fortnight before the young woman was brought in.'

After Virtue Hall, Thomas Colley testified that he and his wife had parted from Elizabeth Canning in Houndsditch at 'about a quarter or very near half an hour after nine o'clock' on the evening of New Year's Day. Then Mrs Canning gave evidence of her daughter's reappearance at quarter after ten o'clock at night, on the day before King Charles's Martyr-dom, and how she fell into a fit and how her daughter was also liable to fall into fits – sometimes for seven or eight hours, sometimes for three or four – and that she was then reduced to no more than a new-born babe. John Wintlebury recounted how he had gone to Mrs Canning's house when he heard of her daughter's return, and how Elizabeth had told him that she felt very bad and how she had been taken to somewhere where she could see the Hertfordshire coach go by and that he, Wintlebury, had not asked her many questions as she was in a great flurry.

One after another, the Canning friends – and friends of their friends – testified to Elizabeth's dramatic reappearance in Aldermanbury Postern on the night of 29th January, of her good character and of the goings on during the expedition to Enfield Wash. Mr Adamson, in particular, gave a vivid account of his part in the proceedings: riding back from Mother Wells's house to the coach, to ask Elizabeth Canning about the hay in the loft, and how he carried her – weak and emaciated – like a child in his arms to examine the house and identify Mary Squires and Virtue Hall. Finally, there was the testimony of Sutherland Backler, the apothecary. He told how he examined Elizabeth Canning on 30th January and how she was 'extremely low and weak' and how he could 'scarcely hear her speak, her voice was so low, and her pulse scarcely to be felt, with cold sweats'.

The revelations of the sufferings of the frail serving-maid wrung the hearts of the courtroom spectators and increased still further the hostility of the mob against her gipsy persecutors and the villains who were willing to testify on their behalf. Defence witnesses were attacked as they tried to enter the Sessions House; Fortune Natus and his wife were battered by the angry mob; Susannah Well's neighbours, who had come to speak on her behalf, were turned away. Her elder daughter, Elizabeth, was recognized and the shout went up against 'Mother Wells's daughter' and her half-brother, John Howit, when they tried to enter the court.

Only three defence witnesses passed unmolested and that because they were unrecognised as such in their rustic garbs. John Gibbons, William Clarke and Thomas Greville had travelled up from Dorset and Wiltshire to give evidence for Mary Squires.

John Gibbons told the court that he lived at Abbotsbury, six miles from Dorchester. He was master of an inn, The Old Ship. On 1st January of that year the prisoner Squires came into the inn with her son, George, and her daughter, Lucy. She carried handkerchiefs, lawns, muslins and checks to sell about the town. Mary Squires and her two children stayed at his inn until the 9th January.

William Davy asked Gibbons how long he had kept The Old Ship at Abbotsbury.

'I have kept it two years, come Lady Day.'

'Look at that woman,' Davy said, pointing to the old gipsy woman in the dock. 'Are you sure that is she?'

'I am sure it is,' came the reply.

'By what do you recollect the day?' asked Mr Stow in his cross-examination.

'There came an exciseman to officiate there for one John Ward that was sick, and I put the day of the month down when he came; the excise office is kept at my house; the man that came was Andrew Wicks, or Wick.'

'Did you see the prisoner sell any of these goods you mentioned?'

'No, I did not; they offered to sell them to me, and others; my wife bought two check gowns.'

William Clarke, a cordwainer, and another Abbotsbury man, testified that he saw the old gipsy woman on the road, on 10th January last. They walked some way together and parted at Ridgeway-foot, four miles from Abbotsbury. Like John Gibbons, Clarke had a particular reason for noting the date: he had entered in his accounts that he had carried out goods on that day to Portesham.

'Have you your book with you?' demanded Mr Stow.

'No, I have not; but I cannot forget the day, because I do not go so often.'

'Which way were they going?'

'They were making for London; they talked so.'

'Did they give you any account of what place they were bound next?'

'They did not; they lodged at this man's house at Abbotsbury,' Clarke replied, pointing to John Gibbons.

'Did you see them there?'

'I did, on the 1st of January: I commonly go there of an evening, to have a pot of liquor.'

Thomas Greville, landlord of The Lamb at Coombe [Bissett], three miles from Salisbury, swore that he saw Mary Squires in his public house on the 14th January. She stayed one night. Like the other West Country witnesses, Greville had a particular reason for noticing the old gipsy: on that day there had been a carpenter staying at his house who had spent 'the biggest part of his money' and had had to be put out, 'it being a Sunday night'. Greville ejected him three times, after

35

which the carpenter went over to another house and pawned his axe.

The next witness appeared belatedly for the prosecution. His evidence flatly contradicted the testimonies of the three defence witnesses. He sold fish and oysters at Waltham Cross and Theobolds and was often near Enfield Wash; he knew Mary Squires by sight. The last time he saw her was when she was taken at Susannah Wells's house and he had seen her 'every day up and down, before she was taken.'

'Are you certain of that?' Mr Stow demanded.

'I am, that I saw her three weeks before, that she walked into people's houses, pretending to tell fortunes. She told me mine once.'

The fishmonger's testimony was the final bizarre turn of evidence in the trial of Mary Squires and Susannah Wells, for Mrs Wells's witnesses had failed to fight their way into the courtroom and she had no lawyer. Her case was hopeless; her defence two simple sentences.

'As to my character, it is but an indifferent one; I had an unfortunate husband who was hanged. I never saw the young woman [Elizabeth Canning] till they came to take us up; and, as to Squires, I never saw her above a week and a day before we were taken up.'

*　　*　　*

The jury found Mary Squires and Susannah Wells guilty.

Five days later the two women were hauled back to the Sessions House for sentence: Mother Wells for branding on the thumb – she screamed horribly while it was done – and six months in Newgate Gaol; the old gipsy to death by hanging.

Mary Squires spoke before she was sentenced.

'On New Year's Day I lay at Coombe at the Widow Greville's house; the next day I was at Stoptage; there were some people who were cast away, and they came along with me to a little house on the top of the moor, and drank there; there were my son and daughter with me. Coming along Pophamlane, there were some people raking up dung. I drank at the second ale-house in Basingstoke on the Thursday in the New Year week. On the Friday I lay at Bagshot Heath, at a little tiny house on the heath. On the Saturday, I lay at Old Brentford at Mrs Edwards's, who sells greens and small beer. I could have told this before, but one pulled me, and another pulled me, and would not let me speak. I lay at Mrs Edwards's on the Sunday and Monday; and on the Tuesday or Wednesday after, I came from thence to Mrs Wells's house at Enfield.'

6

Sir Crisp to the Rescue

ELIZABETH CANNING WAS the talk of London as the damp February days lengthened into the clear, cold March of 1753. The newspapers were full of her. Pamphlets describing her ordeal at Enfield Wash were in all the coffee houses; fictitious versions of Mary Squires's expected speech at Tyburn gallows were already being scribbled. Public indignation was whipped up by news of another gipsy atrocity: a robbery on Norwood Common in which the victim, Little Jemmy ('a poor man who cries sticks about the streets'), was robbed of three pence and used most cruelly, by five gipsies, who stamped on his stomach.

She was fêted, not only by the mob, but by respectable citizens who trooped to the Royal Exchange, Lloyds and St Dunstan's coffee houses to hand over their donations for the 'benefit'. They talked of nothing else in Ranelagh Pleasure Gardens and at Vauxhall. Even noblemen and persons of quality gossiped about the scullery-maid. The customers of White's Chocolate House, in St James's, requested her presence – and closely questioned her – before handing over a purse of thirty golden guineas. The total collected, it was said, was not far short of three hundred pounds and enabled Elizabeth

Canning to move to more comfortable accommodation in the house of Mr Marshall, the cheesemonger, of Aldermanbury.

Not everyone was content with the turn of the events. Sir Crisp Gasgoyne certainly was not. And neither was Mr Justice Gundry. They both had doubts about the verdict on Mary Squires and Susannah Wells. Sir Crisp had been outraged by the courtroom mob preventing witnesses from giving evidence. More than anything, he had been impressed by the Dorset and Wiltshire men who had sworn to the presence of Mary Squires at Abbotsbury and at Coombe when the prosecution witnesses had placed her at Enfield Wash.

If what they swore was false, Sir Crisp reasoned, "twas easily detected, and if true, this woman could not be guilty.' Neither, he argued, would they travel more than a hundred miles 'to foreswear themselves on behalf of this miserable object.'

Accordingly, letters were dispatched to Dorset: the first to the Vicar of Abbotsbury, written, at the Lord Mayor's direction, by Thomas Ford of Aldermanbury:

SIR,

I am honoured with the Commands of my Lord Mayor, and in his Preface I write to you upon the following occasion.

At this present Session, *Mary Squires*, an old Gipsy, was convicted of robbing *Elizabeth Canning*, on the 2nd January last, at *Enfield* in *Middlesex*.

The principal Witnesses in Support of the Prosecution were *Canning* herself, and one *Virtue Hall*, who gave positive Evidence against her.

In her Defence, *John Gibbons* and *William Clark* of your Parish as positively attested, that she, with her Son *George* and Daughter *Lucy*, came there the 1st of January, quartered at Gibbons' House, and stayed there till the 9th, selling Lawns, Handkerchiefs, Cheques and the like.

The Convict is so very remarkable, 'tis as impossible that any of the Witnesses can be mistaken in her Person, as that their different Accounts can be true.

She is at least 70, tall, and stoops; her face is long and meagre, her Nose very large, her Eyes very full and dark, her Complexion remarkably swarthy, and her under Lip of prodigious Size.

Where the Perjury lies is a Question, you, Sir, by Enquiry in your Parish, may easily resolve; the Facts sworn to your Parishioners being such, as must be notoriously true, or notoriously false.

If true, God forbid she should suffer; and if false, those Men ought not to escape with Impunity.

The End of this Letter carries with it so good an Excuse for the Trouble it may give you – 'tis needless to add to it.

If there is the Life of a Fellow-Creature in one Scale, there is the Character of a young Girl in the other, whose Suffering, if real, deserves universal Pity.

The sacred Function you bear is a Security to his Lordship for your Humanity, and your Justice.

To your Account, you will be pleased to add, what are the Characters of *Gibbons* and *Clarke*.

I am Sir,
Your most humble Servant

T. FORD

London, 24 Feb. 1753.
Please to direct to me in *Aldermanbury*.

The Vicar penned his reply on 5th March. The gipsies had been seen in Abbotsbury in early January: one parishioner, who had known Mary Squires for upwards of thirty years, had spotted them at the house of John Gibbons – several times – between 1st and 9th January; George and Lucy Squires were said to have been dancing almost every night with the young people of the town.

The Lord Mayor was not the only one to be dabbling in Dorset: Sir Crisp's companion on the bench, Mr Justice Gundry, had been enquiring in Abbotsbury. His clerk, Mr Bun, wrote to the Under-Sheriff of Dorsetshire and, in reply, received an interesting package of papers.

The Under-Sheriff, confirmed that he had seen Gibbons and Clarke. He judged them to be very honest men who 'would not have given evidence had it not been true'. One of them, William Clarke, had fallen in love with Lucy Squires, the Deputy-Sheriff discovered, and had followed the gipsies to Ridgeway and stayed with them there for a day or two. Another letter was signed by fifteen prominent inhabitants of Abbotsbury – churchwardens, overseers of the poor, the schoolmaster, farmers, a mercer, a tything man – all certifying that Mary, George and Lucy Squires were well known to them, that the witnesses Gibbons and Clarke were of good character and that the gipsies had stayed at The Ship Inn from, 'or about', the first day of January for nine days. Also on Mr Bun's desk was an affidavit, given and signed before the Mayor of Dorchester, by six Abbotsbury men, who had walked twenty miles to do so. They too testified that Mary Squires, and her two children, were well known to them and that they had seen them in Abbotsbury on 1st January, where they had continued for another nine days: 'as can be proved at least by one hundred other Persons in *Abbotsbury* aforesaid'.

The Lord Major received a letter signed by six inhabitants of Coombe, in the County of Wiltshire, certifying that: 'Thomas Greville . . . is a very honest Man, and always bore a good Character; and we, who have set our Names hereunder, do believe that the Gypsy-woman was at Coombe at the same Time, according to Evidence.'

*   *   *

Someone else was also ferreting about on the track of the Aldermanbury scullery-maid.

Dr John Hill was an extraordinary man, even by the inflated standards of the mid-eighteenth century: apothecary, playwright, professional botanist, journalist and quack. He could produce, with marvellous speed, book after book, as well as churning out – seven days a week – a scandalous newspaper column 'The Inspector'. A witty, unbalanced and quarrelsome man, his satirical and scurrilous writings involved him in frequent squabbles. He had quarrelled with the comedian Woodward, was publicly thrashed by an Irish gentleman at Ranelagh, and had gained the enmity of the actor David Garrick, who retaliated with the well-known epigram:

For physic and farces, his equal there scare is,
His farces are physic, his physic a farce is.

John Hill, 'The Inspector', had also squabbled with Henry Fielding in his *Covent Garden Journal*. Fielding won the day, the year before, gloating that 'this *hill* was only a paltry *dunghill*, and had long before been levelled with the dirt'.

Henry Fielding's part in the Canning case presented a perfect opportunity for John Hill. It came to him on the evening of 6th March, when he visited a Mr Prentice, manufacturer of 'iron-pear-tree water', with whom he had business. Among Mr Prentice's guests in Parliament Street that night was a Westminster magistrate, Mr Justice Lediard. John Hill had already sniffed out that the Lord Mayor was making discreet enquiries in Dorset and Wiltshire about the Canning case. At Mr Prentice's house, he discovered from Mr Lediard the whereabouts of Virtue Hall and, what is more, that she had shown signs of remorse and a willingness to speak about the events at Enfield Wash.

John Hill called on Sir Crisp Gascoyne that evening with the news that Virtue Hall had been taken to the Gatehouse prison by Canning's friends. She was now living there – although not under confinement – but had, according to Justice Lediard, expressed uneasiness about her testimony at the trial of the old gipsy woman and Mother Wells.

Sir Crisp had several 'gentlemen of distinction' with him in the Mansion House that evening; it was their opinion, as well as Sir Crisp's, that Virtue Hall should immediately be sent for. Accordingly, Sir Crisp dispatched Mr White, the Marshal's man, to fetch her.

Mr White returned within two hours, Virtue Hall in tow, together with one of the gaoler's servants, and – to Sir Crisp's huge astonishment – a contingent of Elizabeth Canning's friends. White told Sir Crisp that none of them had been at the Gatehouse prison when he was there, but they must have got wind of what was happening, for they were waiting outside the Mansion house when he got back. He said that Canning's friends had called out: 'Be sure, Virtue, remember what you swore before, and stand to it.'

Sir Crisp started his examination of Virtue Hall there and then. He spoke gently and admonished her to speak the truth. But he could get very little from her, only 'Yeses' and 'Noes'. Even these were extracted with every sign of horror and distress – and little indication of the truth.

Sir Crisp thought it best to take Virtue Hall to another room. A guest, Sir John Phillips, went along as a witness. The little Enfield whore burst into tears as soon as they were on their own and confessed that all she had sworn previously was false. She had not spoken in the other room, because 'the friends of Canning were by'.

Sir Crisp gave Virtue Hall quarter of an hour alone to recover herself. When he and Sir John returned, she was ready to speak.

'Canning never came into the house,' Virtue Hall confessed. She said that Fortune Natus and his wife slept in the room in which Canning had sworn that she had been kept and that Squires and her family had arrived only eight days before she was taken up. The accounts that she had given in her examination by Justice Tyshmaker and Justice Fielding had been false.

*   *   *

Virtue Hall was brought to the soaring splendour of the great new Mansion House on the following day for more questioning by the Lord Mayor – and anyone else who cared to interrogate her. Elizabeth Canning and her supporters were there in force.

They made a strange contrast, the demure heroine of Aldermanbury Postern and the sullen prostitute from Enfield Wash.

Again, Virtue Hall was asked how it was that she now foreswore herself? Her answer was the same: 'when I was at Mr Fielding's I at first spoke the truth, but was told it was not the truth. I was terrified and threatened to be sent to Newgate, and prosecuted as a felon, unless I should speak the truth.'

The allusion to Henry Fielding was music to John Hill's ears.

Virtue Hall was asked how it was that she could so accurately confirm Elizabeth Canning's evidence?

'I heard Canning's story at Mrs Wells's the day we were taken up, afterwards at Justice Tyshmaker's and afterwards from several other persons.'

She had also stood near Elizabeth Canning at the trial and had heard her evidence again before she was called upon to give her own.

Virtue Hall survived the questioning, including a close interrogation by a member of the Enfield Wash expedition, Edward Rossiter, concerning Elizabeth Canning's white apron, which she mentioned in her evidence. Hall denied that she had seen the bedgown, which Elizabeth was wearing when she reappeared in Aldermanbury Postern, but identified the black pitcher from which Elizabeth Canning said she drank when she was locked in Mother Wells's hay-loft.

Sir Crisp was as impressed with Virtue Hall's performance as Henry Fielding had been by Elizabeth Canning's: 'the girl then went through a strict examination of two hours, with that deportment, consistency, and freedom (the characters of truth) that all who were present (Canning's friends excepted) seemed convinced; indeed there could not now want further occasion of conviction.'

A curious incident occurred at the end of the proceedings when Elizabeth Canning started to fold up the bedgown that she claimed to have brought from Enfield Wash.

'Child, you must not take it away with you,' Sir Crisp warned her in a kindly way.

44

'Yes, my lord,' Sir Crisp heard her reply. 'I must, *it is my mother's.*'

Like everything else in the Canning case, this damning remark was disputed. Edward Rossiter recalled that Elizabeth Canning had said: 'I must *take them* to my mother's.'

But its significance was not lost on John Hill. He had found a very effective stick to beat his enemy Fielding.

7

Witnesses Galore

HENRY FIELDING SOON got wind of what had been happening in the Mansion House – and of John Hill's hand in events. He reacted with characteristic decisiveness, summoning Elizabeth Canning to his house in Bow Street and there 'endeavoured by all means in my power to sift the truth out of her, and to bring her to confession if she was guilty'. According to Fielding: 'she persisted in the truth of the evidence that she had given, and with such an appearance of innocence, as persuaded all present of the justice of her cause'.

He made no attempt to re-examine Virtue Hall for 'in truth she deserves no credit at all'. Mr Fielding was only interested in 'evidence of fact which alone is always safely to be depended upon, as it is alone incapable of a lie'.

Fielding was particularly impressed that Hall and Canning had never set eyes on one another before Canning had arrived at Mother Wells's house. So it would have been impossible for the two women to 'lay this story together'. Virtue Hall's statement – that he had bullied and threatened her – was 'a most impudent falsehood' and her claim that she heard Elizabeth Canning give her evidence was 'impossible' and 'can be proved to be another notorious falsehood, by a great number of witnesses of indisputable credit'.

Furthermore, Fielding argued, 'why did not the gipsy woman and Wells produce the evidence of Fortune Natus and his wife in the defence at their trial, since that evidence, as they well knew, was so very strong in their behalf, that had the jury believed it, they must have been acquitted?'

Above all, it was Elizabeth Canning's simplicity and obvious innocence that so moved and impressed Henry Fielding: 'Nor will I quit this case, without observing the pretty incident of the mince-pie; which, as it possibly saved this poor girl's life, so doth the intention of carrying it home to her little brother, serve very highly to represent the goodness, as well as the childishness and simplicity of her character; a character so strongly imprinted in her countenance, and attested by all her neighbours.'

Fielding was reassured by 'a great number of affidavits corroborating the whole evidence of Canning'. They were by 'unquestionable witnesses, and sworn before three worthy Justices of the County of Middlesex, who live in the neighbourhood of Enfield Wash', and flatly contradicted 'the alibi defence of the gipsy woman'.

*   *   *

Enfield witnesses were essential for the Canningites or Canaanites (as Elizabeth's supporters were now known), to outface the increasing array of testimonies from the West, of which the Lord Mayor kept them fully informed. And they lost no chance to bluster and whip up anti-gipsy feelings in handbills, newspaper articles and advertisements, threatening that: 'attempts to screen *such offenders*, cannot fail to awake the publick Attention, to bring the Rest of those *Miscreants* (and all such Persons, who, in Defiance of all Laws, human and divine, shall dare to become Partakers of their Crimes by Perjury) to Justice.'

The *Publick Advertiser*, of March 19th, 1753, predicted that: 'notwithstanding the many puffs on the other side of the question the friends of Elizabeth Canning flatter themselves, her case will not be attended with that intricacy as is insinuated; and the World in due time will be acquainted with the true state of her case'. The readers would, in addition, be informed who 'the *King of the Gipsies* was.' [He was – as any broadsheet reader would know – Sir Crisp Gascoyne, who, if anything, was now more unpopular than 'the King of the Jews' (Sir William Calvert) who had also incurred unpopularity by his support for the 'Jew Bill', enabling the naturalization of some individual Jews.]

A few days later, the *Gazetteer* was pitching into gipsies ('a counterfeit kind of rogues, who, disguising themselves in strange habits, smearing their faces and bodies, and framing to themselves a canting unknown language'), pronouncing dire warning against 'espousers and upholders of gipsies' (a thinly veiled threat against the 'Egyptians', as the supporters of the Enfield gipsies were now known) and inveighing against 'fortune tellers, impostors, bawds, whores, thieves, robbers, smugglers, murderers and plunderers at shipwrecks'.

The Canningite propagandist was John Myles, 'Attorney of Birchin Lane', who had replaced Mr Salt as Elizabeth Canning's solicitor. A wily and resourceful lawyer, Myles missed no opportunity to defend his client's position – by pamphlet, rumour and advertisement – to expose the 'various scandalous and malicious falsehoods raised and reported of Elizabeth Canning by several persons, particularly by Mr Hill and his associates.' What is more, Myles fulminated: 'I do hereby take upon me to discern that several persons, for the sake of justice only, are daily informing me of several material circumstances, fully corroborating her unhappy case.'

John Myles was, in fact, scouring the Middlesex countryside for anyone who would testify that they had seen Elizabeth Canning – or her gipsy kidnappers – within miles of Enfield Wash. And he was having considerable success, for witnesses were flocking to tell of undoubted sightings of the old gipsy woman and of the Aldermanbury girl in the bitter days of January 1753.

A turnpike keeper from the Tottenham road told how his

children brought news from school of a girl who had been 'forced away from her friends near Moorfields to a bad house at Enfield Wash'. After turning this over in his mind, he realized that she must have been the very one he saw – 'at about the fore-end of January' – sobbing and crying at about eleven o'clock of a calm, still night. It was coming from the direction of Newington. Then he saw two men come out of the darkness dragging a woman saying: 'Come along you bitch, you are drunk' and 'Damn the bitch, how drunk she is!' The woman cried bitterly as the men forced her over a stile and then dragged her on, saying: 'Damn you, you bitch, come along, you are drunk.'

The turnpike keeper said that he watched them go on their way towards Enfield, and listened until he could hear them no more. The woman was not tall and was wearing light-coloured clothes. He had not interfered.

A shopkeeper came forward to tell how he was returning home, near Mrs Wells's house, on 29th January. At between four and five o'clock, that afternoon, he saw a woman – 'a miserable poor wretch' – standing in the gateway to a gravel-pit 'near the ten-mile stone'. She wore neither gown, nor stays, nor cap or a hat – only a ragged handkerchief – and a piece of cloth, reaching below her waist, with no apron. The woman had asked him the way to London and would have gone in the wrong direction had he not directed her. He remembered that it was the 29th, because it was the day before a man came – on the 30th – to take up his son for an apprentice.

Another Enfield man said he was chopping rotten bushes outside his house that same afternoon when he saw 'a poor distressed creature come by me out of the common field, from Mrs Wells's ward, for London'.

Then Loomworth Dane, landlord of The Bell, turned up to tell the gentlemen from London that he had seen Mary Squires at Enfield Wash. It was on 'Old Christmas Day': 5th January, according to the new style. [The Julian calendar was not reformed in England until 1752, when eleven superfluous days were lopped from the year so that the 2nd became the 14th day

49

of September.] Loomworth Dane had been at his door, filling a barrow with gravel, to lay in the yard. As the old gipsy walked by, the wind blew up her gown and Dane spotted a huge hole in the heel of her stocking.

One by one the witnesses came forward – or were winkled out. Samuel Storey, a man of independent fortune, said that he saw the gipsy woman on 23rd December, in Turkey Street, Enfield Wash. He remembered the day well, because it was a Saturday before Christmas – a fine frosty morning – and he had been suffering from rheumatism, before he was seized by St Antony's fire [erysipelas] on the following Monday or Tuesday. A farmer was convinced that he had seen Mary Squires in his cow house at Ranton Row, in Enfield, on 13th December: a date he remembered because the day before he had been 'stamping of apples'.

Sarah Star, a farmer's wife, was certain that Mary Squires came to her door – asking if she had any Delft pottery to mend – on the 18th or 19th January, she thought. Then young William Headland – he was twenty years old – turned up to tell how he had discovered a piece of lead from the broken window, through which Elizabeth Canning had escaped, in Mrs Wells's garden: there were traces of blood on it, he said.

John Myles left nothing to chance. Enfield volunteers were shipped off to visit Newgate Gaol to make sure they could recognize Mary Squires. Daniel Bass, a labouring man from Turkey Street, went with eight or nine others from Enfield. Wise Bassett was there as well and found Mary Squires sitting by a fire in a crowded room, still smoking her pipe; and yet more were taken in their turn to gawp at the old gipsy woman in the hell that was Newgate Gaol.

*   *   *

While John Myles was engaged at Enfield, the Lord Mayor was busy in the Mansion House – to exactly opposite effect.

On 12th March 1753, Fortune and Judith Natus were grilled there for two hours. They told Sir Crisp they had lodged with

Susannah Wells for ten weeks before she and Mary Squires were taken up. During all that time (except for one night before Christmas) they had slept in the loft in which Elizabeth Canning claimed she had been confined. Their bed was the hay that was kept there for Mrs Wells's old horse, with a bag of wool for a bolster, and a large piece of blue cloth and some old sacks for their sheeting. Judith Natus said that the pitcher – which Elizabeth Canning swore she had with her in the loft – was in constant use by the families at Mother Wells's. According to Mrs Natus, Mary Squires and her family did not arrive at Enfield Wash until a week and a day before they were taken up. She and her husband had been prevented from giving evidence at the trial of Mary Squires and Susannah Wells by the mob in the Old Bailey Yard.

All this was duly taken down, signed by the labourer and his wife with their marks, and witnessed by Sir Crisp Gascoyne in the Mansion House.

Another Enfield man was also examined by the Lord Mayor on that March day. He testified that he was at Mrs Wells's house on the 18th January to fetch away part of the arm of an inn sign. He found it beneath the foot of the hay bed in which Judith Natus was lying. This information too was taken upon oath, signed and witnessed by Crisp Gascoyne.

Elizabeth Long, Mrs Wells's eldest daughter, gave evidence – which she had been prevented from giving at the Old Bailey by the violence of the mob – and signed it. She said that she lived near her mother's house and went there almost daily. Mary Squires, George and Lucy, now joined by her other daughter, Polly, had arrived on a Wednesday and had been taken away on the Thursday of the following week. Mrs Long said that she had never seen Elizabeth Canning until the day her mother was carted away.

The next day, the chandler's wife from Enfield Wash was brought to the Mansion House. She lived almost opposite Mrs Wells's house and told Sir Crisp that the gipsies came to her shop on the Wednesday of the week before Mary Squires was taken up [i.e. 24th January] and that she *never* saw them at

Enfield before that day. Her statement was carefully copied out and she made her mark on it.

After Mary Larney, came witnesses from Dorset into the Mansion House, still pristine in its newness: a blacksmith and a carpenter eager to swear to the presence of Mary Squires, with George and Lucy, in the first days of January at Abbotsbury.

Then, perhaps most extraordinary of all, there appeared three of Elizabeth Canning's companions from the now famous expedition to Enfield Wash: Gawen Nash, John Hague and Edward Aldridge. Despite any earlier enthusiasms, they now had severe doubts about Canning's story. For one thing, it was very odd that Elizabeth Canning had, at first, not mentioned the pile of hay in the loft and that there was no grate in the room, while she had said there had been. And they had not seen – they now claimed – any sign of the window-frame having been nailed or fastened up, as Canning said it had. Neither had she made any mention of the jackline and pulley in the loft (that communicated, through a hole in the wall, with the kitchen) and from which she could have heard everything that was going on below.

It was all written down – the doubts and misgivings of Messrs Nash, Hague and Aldridge – and duly signed and witnessed by the Lord Mayor of London, on the 23rd March, 1753.

Three days later, another Dorset man walked into the Mansion House. Andrew Wake, the excise collector, told Sir Crisp that he had spent several evenings in Abbotsbury with Mary, George and Lucy Squires in the first frosty days of January. What is more, he could be very particular as to dates for the entries in his excise book gave confirmation.

Then a letter came in from Wiltshire. John Cooper of Salisbury wrote to tell Sir Crisp Gascoyne that he had been asked by Mr Myles to give him accounts of the characters of any of the inhabitants of Coombe who had 'pretended' to see the Squires there. Mr Cooper enclosed the names of seven villagers who claimed to have seen the gipsy family on the 14th

January. He also provided evidence of the good character of Thomas Greville, who had testified at her trial that Mary Squires had been in Coombe on that day.

Mr Cooper wrote again – as previously, in 'the interest of truth' – to provide the Lord Mayor with more of the information that he had gleaned for Mr Myles. He also added his own solution.

My Lord,

Since I sent your Lordship the former Account of the Testimony collected at *Coombe* concerning the old Gypsy-Woman, I had an Opportunity of taking down some additional Evidence on this Matter, which I enclose for your Lordship's Inspection.

I am really surprised, that neither Mr *Fielding*, nor Dr *Hill* suspect that *Elizabeth Canning* might absent herself, to cover the Shame of a Lying-in; and which, if it were the Case, would account for the meagre Condition she returned in, and the Time of her Absence.

I return your Lordship thanks for your good Opinion of me: and I shall be ready to assist as far as I can to bring the strange Affair to light.

I am with due Respect,
   Honoured Sir,
     Your Lordship's most
      obedient humble servant,

JOHN COOPER.

Salisbury 10th April, 1753

P.S. Mr *Miles* had an exact Duplicate of the Testimonies sent your Lordship.

8

Dorset Alibi

THE EVIDENCE WHICH Mr Ford and Mr Bun gleaned for Sir Crisp and Justice Gundry told a very different story from the one that Mr Myles put together about Mary Squires's whereabouts during January, 1753. It is a version that involves dozens of witnesses – scattered half across England – is consistent within itself and, for the most part, can be assembled in sequence like pieces in a jigsaw puzzle. Yet there are perplexing episodes, curious gaps – and total conflict with the evidence of Elizabeth Canning.

If true, it is the story of a journey. A journey – erratic and intermittent – starting in remote wintry countryside on the Somerset-Dorset border, heading down towards the channel coast, before swinging back along highways, open downland and muddy tracks through Dorset, Wiltshire and Hampshire towards London and the frozen Middlesex countryside.

On 29th December, according to the following reconstruction, the gipsies were making for South Perrott: a quiet stone and thatch village beside the River Parrett, which flowed sluggishly from its source a mile eastward along the valley. The Squires were curiously vague about how they came to be in that north-western corner of Dorset. They said that they had

Mary Squires

come from the east – from the 'wilds' [Weald?] of Kent and
from Sussex – had passed close to Shaftesbury, but knew
nothing of nearby Yeovil and, later, could recall nothing of the
other villages on their way.

The gipsies ate and slept at The Red Lion that night. On
the following morning – by their account – they headed south
east and, between eight and nine o'clock, had passed by the
break in the high Dorset plateau, Wynyard's Gap, to reach
The Three Horseshoes. Mary Squires was puffing from the
exertion of the climb when she entered the inn. The landlady's daughter drew a quart of beer, served the gipsies with
bread and cheese and stayed with them for the hour that they
spent at the inn. They asked her how far it was to Litton

[Cheyney] and, as they left, told her that they would return one day.

It was a stiff walk to Litton Cheyney, some eleven miles more across the grey-green Dorset hills. On a fine day, they could have seen Salisbury Plain away to the east, and northwards, across the Mendips and the Bristol Channel, to the distant purple of the Welsh hills. Later, if the day was clear, they might have seen the sea to the south – glittering or leaden – glimpsed between distant cliffs and hills. Their way rolled southward to skirt the eastern ramparts of the earthen fortress that topped Eggardon Hill: the domain of Isaac Gulliver – owner of Higher Eggardon Farm – who controlled the 'Free Trade', with never less than forty or fifty smugglers at his command. Gulliver had planted a clump of trees on Eggardon Hill, as a landmark for the smugglers at sea; his men, who brought contraband on pack ponies, wore a sort of uniform – a smock and powdered wig – for which they were dubbed 'White Wigs' by those who knew them in that part of Dorset.

Later accounts would link the gipsies' presence there with Isaac Gulliver's trade.

From Eggardon, they dropped down between encircling hills, keeping a long grassy ridge on their right, and then slowly climbing again before dropping precipitously into Litton Cheyney, past a comfortable house and cottages – to the sound of running water from the two streams that ran on either side of the village street – and the church of St Mary sitting primly on its knoll.

The village plasterer and tiler was working on the public house (which used to be The Three Horseshoes before it lost its sign) when he spotted the three travellers at about two o'clock that winter afternoon. He had known the 'old woman' for more than thirty years. The publican also knew Mary Squires and her children and prepared a room, which had been newly built on, for them to spend the night.

Next morning, the last of the old year – when sightings of the gipsies at Enfield Wash were claimed – George Squires said that he was shaved by Francis Gladman, a gardener by trade.

Thus smartened, George walked off to Abbotsbury, some five miles to the south east on the coast. He had a clear purpose in so doing, for in Abbotsbury dwelt William Clarke, cordwainer – Lucy Squires's sweetheart – who was waiting for news of George's dark-haired sister. George Squires slept that night in Clarke's house in Abbotsbury.

Back at Litton Cheyney, Mary and Lucy Squires were enjoying the modest festivities which were the custom of that village on New Year's morning. Francis Gladman and the other members of the band rang a peal on the church bells and, afterwards, were given some ale and a jug of cider for so doing. They took the cider to the public house to 'have something put into it' [gin?] and came across Mary Squires sitting by the fire, smoking her pipe.

The cider, and whatever was put into it, evidently loosened Mr Gladman's tongue – and wits. He sat down next to Mary Squires, treating her with the patronizing superiority of the peasant for the Romany. Did she read fortunes, he asked.

'No,' came the untruthful reply. 'I am no fortune teller.'

'Can you talk Spanish?' Gladman enquired; assuring the old gipsy woman that he was sure he had 'seen her abroad somewhere or other'.

Again, Mrs Squires replied that she could not.

'Can you talk Portuguese?' Gladman persisted.

'No.'

'Nor French?'

'No,' came the reply.

'Nor Dutch?'

'No!'

An elderly rustic butted in.

'You must cant to her,' he said. 'Talk gipsy to her and she'll answer you.'

Gladman, however, favoured a direct approach. 'You are one of the scamps,' he said.

'No,' replied Mary Squires wearily, 'I am no scamp.'

And that was all that Francis Gladman could elicit from the

old gipsy that morning. It was left to a younger customer to volunteer her name.

Mary Squires could barely have been listening as Francis Gladman nattered away at her side in John Hawkins's parlour; she was inwardly fussing because George had not returned from Abbotsbury. In the end she could bear it no longer and marched off on her own – at about the time that Elizabeth Canning was setting out from Aldermanbury Postern – to discover what was amiss.

But she did not find George – she must have taken a different route.

By his account, he reappeared in Litton shortly after she left, with William Clarke in tow, bearing a brace of fowls that he had bought in the village, at sixpence each, which the obliging publican boiled for their dinner. The birds were eaten between two and three o'clock, on Mary Squires's return from her fruitless quest to Abbotsbury. The four of them, Mary Squires, George, Lucy and William Clarke, finally left for Abbotsbury – a largish village of thatched stone houses and narrow winding streets, close by Chesil Beach – sometime after three o'clock on New Year's afternoon 1753, as dusk was falling in Litton Cheyney.

They stayed at The Old Ship in Abbotsbury. The landlord knew Mary Squires of old and was expecting the gipsies as they emerged from the evening darkness.

There was much merriment at the inn that night. Melchizedeck Arnold (a blacksmith who could also turn his hand to cider making) played his fiddle for the dancing. John Ford – a carpenter – was there in the parlour and in high good humour. He shook Mary Squires by the hand, drank a round with George – and kissed Lucy. William Clarke danced with Lucy and George with the landlord's daughter. One of the guests – a weaver – could not remember who danced with whom that night, so many were on the floor; Mary Squires sat by the fireside smoking her pipe and enjoying the fun until close on midnight.

The revels at The Old Ship at Abbotsbury continued,

intermittently, for more than a week. An exciseman who lodged in the same room as George Squires, joined in when he could during those cold January days. It snowed that week and George Squires lent the exciseman his greatcoat. The village schoolmaster also lodged at The Old Ship. He rolled up from Devonshire (where he had been visiting his sick wife) later in the week and got badly befuddled one evening.

The Squires's funds were now running low, and all that was left to sell was a couple of waistcoats and a length of cloth (worth about 3/6d).

Whether for this – or another reason – George Squires, Lucy and their mother left, according to Abbotsbury witnesses, on Tuesday, 9th January, in company with Lucy's young man. They headed across the fields that morning to Portesham, just two miles to the east of Abbotsbury and away from the sea. There they stopped to discover what progress the Portesham tailor had made with the clothes he was making for William.

They slept at The Chequer that night.

Between nine and ten o'clock on the following morning, the three gipsies and William Clarke set out in driving rain, heading due east along the grey escarpment of the downs past the hamlet of Waddon, crossing the gap in the grassy ramparts above Coryates, along by Friar Waddon Hill to Upwey and then on to Ridgeway to arrive before eleven o'clock. They made for The Sloop Aground, where there was some commotion about the death of a horse, which had been taken sick on the road the previous day, and had died before dawn. Its owner – a woman who had been on her way to Weymouth market – had asked that it should be skinned, for sixpence, by the Ridgeway blacksmith who was at his gruesome work when the Squires and William Clarke entered the pub yard.

They ate beefsteaks for dinner, between one and two o'clock, sharing them with a turnip seller from Abbotsbury. George Squires borrowed six shillings from William Clarke that afternoon, for he was still worried at the lack of silver in his pocket. Lucy parted from her sweetheart at four o'clock. Before he rode off into the gathering dusk, William Clarke made her promise that she would send a letter to him as soon as she possibly could.

Mary Squires, George and Lucy stayed on at The Sloop Aground. George evidently had a restless night, for the landlord woke to find him – with his old mother – standing at his bedside. Did he want a waistcoat? It would be going cheap. They were short of money, George explained. The landlord replied that he had never had such a waistcoat in his life nor did he want one. He agreed, nevertheless, to take the length of cloth 'for the reckoning', on the promise of George Squires and his mother that they would send, or bring to him, the money that he was owed.

The Squires left The Sloop Aground early in the morning of Thursday, 11th January, 1753.

* * *

Somewhere at about this time – exactly when is uncertain – the Squires said that they received news from Mary's other daughter, Polly. Polly had gone into Kent, to nurse an aunt, but she was now ill herself and was lying in London – apparently in desperate need of help. How this news was relayed to the Squires in Dorset is far from clear – as George later admitted – for his sister could not write and had been given no addresses to which to forward letters that might have been written for her. Very curiously, he also claimed that he could not recall where – or when – Polly's letter had arrived, even whether it had arrived before or after they had stayed at Abbotsbury; perhaps more peculiarly, he could not remember the name of the place at which he had left her in Kent.

But whatever the circumstances surrounding Polly Squires's illness, and the carrying of the news of it to Dorset, the Squires made all speed from Ridgeway. Their road was the old Roman one running – straight as a die – three and a half miles north-north-east to Dorchester. The gipsies' way then skirted the marshy eastern corner of the town, aptly called Fordington, where the River Frome faced them.

It was a perilous passage to attempt the swollen waters that morning. The landlord of The Coach and Horses at Fordington, said they arrived, 'in the forenoon betwixt the hours of eight and eleven'. He saw the miller's boy bring a horse for Lucy to ride across the swollen ford, for which service George Squires bought him a pint of beer. His mother was less fortunate and the landlord watched as the old woman 'lifted up her coats and went through the water'.

Once across the swollen river the gipsies made surprisingly rapid speed, striking out through rolling country to the north east. Their route was most probably to the north of the present London road to Blandford, which in those days ran close to Waterston Manor (that in Hardy's imagination would become Bathsheba Everdene's farmhouse in *Far From The Madding Crowd*), touching Milton Abbey and Winterbourne Strickland.

According to George Squires's account, the three gipsies passed through Blandford and trudged on into the night. By the next day, Friday 12th January, Squires said that they were at a place called Tawney [Thorney?] Down, where 'we went into a little ale house on the road, and had some bread and cheese, and a pint of beer'.

By the afternoon they were not far from the Wiltshire border. Mary Squires was, by this time, very tired; they had walked not less than twenty-six miles since leaving Ridgeway the day before. Yet she found them somewhere to sleep that night. She trudged wearily into a farmyard at the village of Chettle and begged lodging from a thresher, who was standing at his barn door.

'Have you anyone belonging to you?' the thresher asked.

'None but a couple of children,' the old gipsy replied and then called over her shoulder. 'Why don't you come along?'

They slept that night on clean oat straw in an outhouse. The thresher let them stay – as it was raining so hard – until they were ready to leave at between ten and eleven o'clock the next morning.

The gipsies followed the coach road towards Salisbury. By mid-afternoon they had travelled more than ten miles north east into rolling, open country on the Wiltshire border and at about four o'clock they squelched into the straggling downland village of Martin. There they used the same ruse as they had at Chettle to secure lodging: Mary Squires appeared first, banging at Farmer Thane's door, and then, almost as an afterthought – when things were going well – George and Lucy materialised at her elbow. Again, they slept in a barn. That evening, one of the farm servants saw 'the old woman in master's house by the fire, and her daughter was joining [mending] china for them.'

The Squires started out at around eight o'clock the next morning, Sunday, 14th January. A maltster from Coombe saw them. George Squires was in front and, 'half a dozen luggs [some 28 yards] behind him', was 'the old gentlewoman' holding on to her daughter's hand. They were also spotted at about one o'clock coming into the village and again, at two o'clock, by a customer sitting in the parlour of The Lamb, in Coombe.

The three gipsies left The Lamb at seven o'clock on the morning of Monday, 15th January, 1753. After that we know nothing of their movements until three days later, when George Squires's testimony and the evidence of witnesses, places them forty miles on at Basingstoke in Hampshire. Squires's reticence – or amnesia – for those three days, after his detailed recollections of the earlier part of the journey, is only equalled by the silence, and confusion, concerning the gipsies' movements before their arrival at South Perrott on 29th December.

Whatever the reasons for this – and they will be considered later – the scent only grows warm again with the clue from Mary Squires's outburst before her death sentence at the Old Bailey (that she was at Coombe and then at 'Stoptage' [Stockbridge?] before Basingstoke), George's testimony and the evidence of the landlady of The Spread Eagle at Basingstoke.

According to her, Mrs Squires arrived at the inn, with George and Lucy, on 18th January. She was sure of the date, because it was the one on which she penned a letter for Lucy Squires, to her sweetheart at Abbotsbury.

Lucy's letter became a crucial piece of evidence. Unfortunately, it was flawed because the final number of the date was missing. It was later held that it had not been written in 1753 at all.

The letter was dispatched 'To the posthouse in Dorchester, to be directed to Abbotsbury for Mr William Clarke, cord-wainer.'

Basingstoke, Jan 18,175* [the number is torn off]

Sir; this with my kind love and service to you and all your family, hoping you are all in good health, as I be at present. This is to acquaint you that I am very uneasy for your troublesome journey, hoping you received no illness after your journey; so no more at present from your most obedient and humble servant,

LUCY SQUIRES

I desire to hear from you as soon as possible. Direct for Lucy Squires at Brentford, near London. George and mother give their compliments to you, and all your family.

The Squires were unable to stay at The Spread Eagle that night for all the rooms were taken. So they had a pint or two of beer, ate some bread and walked for another couple of miles to Old Basing to find somewhere to sleep. On the next day, they travelled to Bagshot, and spent the night there, and then on to Brentford, where they lodged at the house of a shopkeeper. She remembered their stay with her because a neighbour's child was christened at that time, which gave the date as around 22nd January, 1753.

By the shopkeeper's reckoning, the Squires came to her on Saturday [i.e. 20th January]. The next day – by her account – George went off to London to fetch his other sister, Polly, who was then staying with a relative, Samuel Squires, a customs officer who lived at White Hart Yard. George returned with

Polly to Brentford on the following day, that is on the day of the christening which the shopkeeper remembered [i.e. 22nd January]. According to her, they must have left her house on 23rd January: 'they went all away together on the Tuesday morning towards London'. This tallies with their appearance, later that day, at about four o'clock ('a little before candle lighting') at Seven Sisters, in Tottenham, where they called at the sign of The Two Brewers, asking for a night's lodging. The landlord recognised Mary Squires – for 'she was a woman not common to be seen' – and recollected that he had met her three years before. But there was no room at The Two Brewers that night and he directed the gipsies to a nearby farmhouse where they slept. The following morning, of Wednesday, 24th January they headed towards Edmonton and then on to Cheshunt, from where they were directed to Mrs Wells's at Enfield Wash.

And that was the story, which Mr Bun and Mr Ford gleaned for the Lord Mayor of London and Justice Gundry, of Mary Squires and her children, in January, 1753.

9

The Dunghill and 'The Inspector'

EVENTUALLY THE Lord Mayor was convinced: the gipsies were innocent; Elizabeth Canning had lied.

Now the matter must be laid before the King. Evidence was collated, the testimonials and certificates bundled. A memorial [memo] to the King was composed and signed by Sir Crisp Gascoyne.

On 10th April, George II granted six weeks respite for the execution of Mary Squires, and was 'graciously pleased' to refer the consideration of the evidence – from both sides – to Lord Hardwicke, the Lord Chancellor, and the Attorney- and Solicitor-Generals.

The tide was running against the Canningites. But John Myles was determined to stem it. On 20th April, while His Majesty's legal representatives were still scratching their heads, he appeared in Dorchester, armed with a warrant indicting – for perjury – the witnesses who had testified for Mary Squires. Then he headed for Abbotsbury with a posse of three, carrying small swords, pistols and blunderbusses.

Myles and his supporters made for The Old Ship. They arrested John Gibbons – loftily brushing aside the protests of the Abbotsbury constable – then collected Lucy Squires's young man, William Clarke, and took the two men back to Dorchester to a Justice of the Peace. Bail was offered for the Abbotsbury men. But there was a legal nicety: the warrant made no mention of *where* the perjury was supposed to have been committed. The matter could only be settled in London Myles maintained, using this as an excuse to take the two men back with him.

Myles made another slip on the warrant for John Gibbons: he gave the wrong first name. Gibbons was accordingly released by the Dorchester Justice. But William Clarke was taken off, by coach, to London by Elizabeth Canning's enterprising lawyer.

John Myles tried every trick to persuade Clarke to recant his evidence. When they arrived in London he kept up the pressure, locking the cordwainer in his own house in Birchin Lane for two days to do so. But Clarke stuck to his story: his sweetheart had been in Dorset – with her mother and brother – and *not* at Enfield Wash, in the early days of January, as Elizabeth Canning had sworn.

Despite all John Myles's efforts William Clarke would not recant: he was granted bail and returned to Abbotsbury.

A month later, on 21st May, 1753, the King's writ was carried to Mary Squires. She had been granted free pardon by George II. Lucy and Polly, with their brother George – who still had a reward on his head for the kidnapping of Elizabeth Canning – went down to Newgate and brought out their mother who they loved so well. Then they went straightaway to the Mansion House to thank the Lord Mayor on bended knees.

In the June Sessions, the bill for perjury – which had been preferred against Elizabeth Canning in April – was considered, as was a counter one from the Canningites (against John Gibbons and William Clarke of Abbotsbury with Thomas Greville, of Coombe Bissett). The grand jury directed that all parties should be tried at the September Sessions: Canning for saying that Mary Squires was at Enfield Wash, when she had been in Abbotsbury and Coombe; the three countrymen for saying that she had been in Abbotsbury and Coombe, when she was at Enfield Wash.

* * *

By this time, public interest in the Canning case was fanned still further, not only by bizarre legal decisions and the violence of the mob against the Lord Mayor, but by a pamphlet war between the Canningites and the Egyptians.

Henry Fielding fired the first broadside for the Canningites with a sixty-two page piece – *A Clear State of the Case of Elizabeth Canning* – published at a price of one shilling.

Fielding opened in very general terms – as became customary in the genre – by extolling the 'tenderness' of English law which 'justly claims a preference to the institutions of all other countries; in some of which a criminal is hurried to execution, with rather less ceremony than is required'. Whereas in 'this happy Kingdom', by contrast, 'it proceeds by slow and regular gradations and requires so many antecedent ceremonies to the ultimate discussion of a court of justice, that so far from being in danger of condemnation without a fair and open trial, every man must be tried more than once before he can receive capital sentence'. Even with such perfection, it was, nevertheless, the duty of every man to act on behalf of injured innocence. Thus, to re-examine the 'merits of causes', in newspapers and pamphlets, is most laudable to ensure fair and legal trial.

After eight pages of such preamble, Henry Fielding descended to the question of the Aldermanbury serving-maid and related her ordeal as she had told it to him in February. As Fielding admits, it was 'a very extraordinary narrative . . . consisting of many strange particulars resembling rather a wild dream than a real fact'. But, after examining the circumstances piece by piece, he accepted it – lock, stock and barrel. For him, 'the weight of evidence ought to be strictly conformable to the weight in probability' and 'the wiser a man is the sooner and easier he will believe'.

67

Much more absurd, according to Mr Fielding, is 'he who will believe no such fact on any evidence whatever', for 'the world are much too inclined to think that the credulous is the only fool; whereas, in truth, there is *another fool* of quite opposite character, who is much more difficult to deal with, less liable to the dominion of reason, and possessed of a frailty more prejudicial to himself and often more detrimental to mankind in general'.

Yet, for all his high-flown justifications, it was Elizabeth Canning herself – 'the goodness, as well as the childishness and simplicity of her character' – which led the author of *Amelia* to fulminate against those who attempted to prevail against her.

An innocent young creature who hath incurred the most cruel and unheard-of injuries, is in danger of being rewarded for them by ruin and infamy; and what must extremely aggravate her case, and will distinguish her misery from that of all other wretches upon earth, is, that she will owe all this ruin and infamy to this strange circumstance, that her sufferings have been beyond what human nature is supposed to be capable of bearing; whilst robbery, cruelty, and the most important of all prejudices, will escape with impunity and triumph; and, therefore, will so escape because the barbarity of the guilty parties hath risen to a pitch of wanton and untempered inhumanity, beyond all possibility of belief.

Henry Fielding's pamphlet was augmented by yet more Canningite propaganda, placed by John Myles in numbered advertisements and handbills that regularly appeared in city coffee houses. There was an account of a terrifying incident in Middlesex, when 'a tall lusty man, who was dressed in a red rug greatcoat' fell upon an inhabitant of Enfield Wash, beating him and kicking him 'on several parts of the body'. The villain had sworn that if his victim had borne witness against the old gipsy and Mother Wells, he would have murdered him. On the 11th May, description was given of another disturbance ('when several persons on horseback, to the number of seven or eight, stopped near the house of Susannah Wells, at Enfield Wash'). There they threatened that if Mary Squires should hang 'they would burn all the people's houses, barns and corn thereabouts'. Account was also given of 'a tall lusty man' (now in 'light coloured clothes, his hat flapped, a black ribbon round the crown, instead of a hat string, with a small stick in his hand') who walked before the house of Susannah Wells threatening the inhabitants with fire ('by reason of which threats several of Elizabeth Canning's witnesses, living thereabouts, were greatly terrified').

There was evidently some scepticism about the incident, for the following announcement appeared in the *Gazetteer* of Wednesday, May 16th, 1753.

No. 19.

As several Persons have doubted the Truth
of this Advertisement, (No. 18) this Notice
is given, that *Affidavits* of the Facts are in
my Hands, and may be *seen*.

JOHN MYLES
Attorney, in *Birchin-lane*.

*   *   *

John Hill now entered the lists for the Egyptians with a counterblast of fifty-two sarcastic pages: *The Story of Elizabeth Canning Considered* ('With Remarks on what has been called, *A Clear State of her Case*, by Mr Fielding; and Answers to the Several Arguments and Suppositions of that Writer'.).

Like his formidable adversary, Hill commenced his pamphlet in low key, explaining that he did not wish to be seen as an interested party – far from it – for: 'whatsoever the malice of little adversaries may wish to propagate on this head', and 'however romantic, and however absurd, such conduct may appear to many', yet he was acting 'only on the principle of real honesty and public utility'. Furthermore (as Dr Hill knew only too well) how improper – 'nay how dishonest' – it was to 'prepossess the public against those whom their country has not yet found guilty of any crime'. But that, most regrettably, was what Mr Fielding had done in defending his reputation – and Elizabeth Canning's – and, therefore, it behoved Dr Hill to put matters to rights, even though it was 'possible that I should by this piece of justice make that man more my enemy than he is at present'.

John Hill commenced his self-imposed task, at the beginning, by dissecting the advertisement in the *Daily Advertiser* which had appeared after 'this *little child*' ('as those who despairing to convince the judgement, attempt the passions of mankind, affect to call her') was said to have been carried away.

Why should Elizabeth Canning have been forcibly taken? She was certainly not handsome and her dress, according to Dr Hill, would not tempt *anyone* to rob her of it. And there was her shriek, which was supposed to have been heard coming from a hackney coach that night. 'Who should know the voice of a servant of no consideration, calling in a strange part of the town from a coach?' And how came it about, Dr Hill wondered, that the person who was supposed to have heard it did not attempt to stop the coach or call other persons to assist him 'for there are enough in the streets at ten o'clock'. And *where*, for that matter, was the coachman ('for coaches do not drive themselves')? Why had he not come forward? If the coach carried her, or if she was dragged to Enfield, then how was it – John Hill demanded – that she passed undetected through the turnpikes?

After casting a sceptical eye over the opening stages of this 'absurd, incredible and most ridiculous story', the man who Henry Fielding called 'Dunghill' turned his attention to the evidence of Virtue Hall: 'false and forged: not in part false, but in the whole . . . the offspring only of her terrors'. A matter about which, Hill boasted, 'no one can speak with more authority than I', for, he wrote, 'it was to myself that she promised the confession'. And who was to blame? '*Fielding*', of course!

Then there were the claims of the 'pretty innocent' as to what happened during her alleged confinement at Enfield Wash. She had said that she was promised 'fine clothes' by her captors, if she would 'go their way'. Who was to provide these, Dr Hill wondered? Certainly, no one in a place where 'everything spoke beggary'. It was 'unnatural, ridiculous and absurd': as was Fielding's account of Elizabeth Canning's changes in appearance during her confinement.

Mr Fielding is challenged directly on the latter point.

The poor girl left her Mother plump: this, Sir, is your account, and this the partridge-phrase by which you express it. She returned you say emaciated and black, this was on the 29th of Jan. and, on 1st of February, she went down to Enfield again: as you say, again. Never were transitions so quick, as have been those of this miraculous girl!; for she was not black at this time, upon this 1st of February. A day or two had made an amazing change; for those who were present tell me, she was at that time red and white like other people.

Dr Hill makes merry at the more obvious discrepancies in Miss Canning's original description of the loft at Mother Wells's house. There were no pictures over the chimney, as she had said. Neither was there any grate: 'so that no one could be guilty of this most housewifely trick of putting a gown in one'. And surely a quantity of hay ('near half a load') was 'too large a matter to have been overlooked and too important to have been forgotten'.

Then there was the point – which had so perplexed Mr Fielding – of what the young woman could possibly have been doing if she was not locked up at Enfield Wash.

Dr Hill had no difficulties on this score:

Where a girl, like this, could be; and how employed during the time; is not difficult to imagine. Not with a lover, say you!

You would be happy, Sir, if all you beg should be allowed you. Not with a lover, Sir! Eighteen, let me remind you, is a critical age; and what would not a woman do, that had made an escape, to recover her own credit, and screen her lover.

You have supposed the girl not *wicked* enough to have devised such a deceit. That, God and her own heart alone can tell; and neither you nor I have right to judge of it. But you add, and this we both may judge of, that you do not suppose her *witty* enough to have invented the story. I give you joy, Sir, of your own wit, for thinking so! I am very far from entertaining a high opinion of the girl's intellect; but such as they are, I think the story tallies with them: none but a fool could have devised so bad a one.

You say 'tis worthy of some writer of romances. I love to hear men talk in character: no one knows better how much wit is necessary to the writing of such books; and, to do justice to your last performance, no man has proved more fully, with how small a share of it, they may be written.

Relentlessly – and with unconcealed glee – John Hill cudgelled away, taking to task his enemy for not allowing that Virtue Hall had heard Elizabeth Canning's evidence before she gave her own, for his high-handed treatment of Judith Natus ('an honest woman, wife of an honest labourer') and for calumny and private prejudice against that most worthy and important man, the Lord Mayor of London.

John Hill belaboured poor Fielding most vigorously in his defence of Sir Crisp Gascoyne.

Who, Sir, are you, that are thus dictating unto the Government? Retire into yourself and know your station. Who is more *capable* or who more *indifferent*, than this generous magistrate. Or has there been among the most violent and misguided of this creature's friends [the Canningites], any man, for I will not suppose you could, but has there been any

man, who has dared to whisper to his own heart a thought
that it were otherwise.

Thus did 'The Inspector' – the man who Henry Fielding
boasted he had 'levelled with the dirt' – wreak his spite.

10

The Rabbit Woman
and the Clergyman

THE PAPER WAR continued through the cold spring and into the summer of 1753. Dr Hill's vitriol was countered by a forty-four page piece (*The Inspector inspected; or Dr Hill's story of Elizabeth Canning examined* by 'Philolagus'). Anonymous offerings appeared (*The truth of the case of Elizabeth Canning fairly stated, The account of Canning and Squires fairly ballanc'd.*).

Then came the first of the medical treatises devoted to the affairs of the Aldermanbury scullery-maid.

The author, Dr Dodd, had colourful origins. He was the son of a Spanish officer, Don Jago Mendozo Vasconcellos de Solis, who, in 1719, fled to England, having killed the Governor of Barcelona's son in a duel and married a Miss Dodd, whose surname he adopted to secure the inheritance of a small estate near Newcastle-upon-Tyne. Dodd entered the navy as a surgeon's mate. When he left, in 1751, he practised in Gough Square, Fleet Street. But Dodd also had ambitions for the stage and as an author. In 1752, he published his first work, *An Essay towards a Natural History of the Herring*. The following year he saw the opportunity to further his literary career, by combining it with his expert knowledge, to launch into the affair which was the talk of London, with: *A Physical Account of the Case of Elizabeth Canning*.

Dr Dodd was firmly convinced of the truth of Elizabeth Canning's story. First, there was the important fact of her fit – when she had been set upon in Moorfields – producing 'fright which might cause an irregular influx of animal spirits, aided by the blow; and besides it was near upon the time of the new moon, which is known to have remarkable powers over epilepsies and convulsions'. Her abduction, according to Dr Dodd, was entirely feasible: 'it must be allowed that two *large* men might be able not only to drag but carry a girl, *barely five feet high*, though well set'.

Then there was the question of her survival for a month on a few scraps of bread and a pitcher of water. The doctor found this entirely plausible. After all, Elizabeth Canning was 'an hearty girl, sanguine, and of a florid countenance, that for many years . . . had scarce taken half a pint of liquid aliment in twenty-four hours, and consequently, was subject to costiveness, and as if she had been predisposed for such an accident, she, for five months before had the common female benefit totally obstructed'. She would – Dr Dodd computed – have consumed an average of three ounces of bread and five pints of water per day. This, he further calculated, would have resulted in weight loss of twenty pounds within twenty-seven days. Furthermore, 'the *hardness*' of her fare would be 'an advantage, in that it was less liable to go off by the stool'. The 'minced-pie' would – of course – have provided additional valuable sustenance.

The fact that Elizabeth Canning made no attempt to escape for such a long period was easily explained in medical terms. 'Fear, we are told, is a passion which, 'til it rises to despair, renders the body cold, jellies the blood and numbs the vital faculties'. Only when she had consumed her provision would 'the fear of death prevail over the fear of death'. This would add 'wings to her flight and support her under its fatigue' as well as 'hindering her from going into any house on the road, lest her persecutors might be there'. All these factors would undoubtedly contribute to the condition in which she returned to her mother, namely: 'weakness, faintness of voice, low pulse, cold sweats, great consumption of body, a livid blackness of the skin, the belly swelled, the head heavy, an obstinate costiveness, and a want of other evacuations'.

Finally, Dr Dodd was at pains to refute malicious reports that Elizabeth Canning had 'been in a salivation' [a treatment for venereal disease by which mercury was administered by a jaw clamp]. The blackness of her skin, in the doctor's opinion, was more likely to have been caused by 'blows, the plague, petechial fever, scurvy or starving' – most probably the latter.

James Solas Dodd's investigation was swiftly followed by another. Daniel Cox, M.D., had a considerable advantage over his predecessor, for he had made several examinations of the object of all the furore. First, on the 30th March, when he called on Mr Marshall – the cheesemonger, in Fore Street – in whose house Elizabeth Canning was living in relative affluence on the funds that were still pouring in from Canningite wellwishers.

Dr Cox interviewed Elizabeth Canning, alone, in Mr Marshall's parlour. As usual, she answered without hesitation.

Had she been regular in her courses? No, she had not had any periods for about five months before she was attacked on New Year's Day. She had taken cold one night – shortly before – when she had been at her washing, and her periods had ceased. Nor had they returned since she had been at home or at Mr Marshall's. After enquiring about the state of her intestines and pressing her closely about her diet at Enfield Wash, Dr Cox departed to consider what he had learned.

He reappeared, early on the Monday morning of 19th April, now bent on enquiry into the state of the shift which she had been wearing when she had escaped from Mother Wells's house. Dr Cox had heard *talk* – especially the Aldermanbury midwife's – on the cleanness of the garment and was determined to pursue the matter.

Mrs Canning was summoned to Mr Marshall's parlour and there gave account of her meetings with the awful Mrs Mayle. She explained how Mrs Mayle had asked to see, and was allowed to examine, the garment; how the midwife deemed it to be free of any evidence of 'commerce with men, nor any distemper, or other discharge', for the shift was 'free from all kind of stains'.

Had the midwife expressed any doubt of the shift being worn so long, asked Dr Cox? Not in the least, Mrs Canning replied. Was it the same shift that her daughter had worn on New Year's Day? Mrs Canning believed that it was. Was there any soil upon the shift and was it dirty enough to have been worn for so many days? It was indeed very dirty at the sleeves and neck, came the reply, but cleaner in the body.

One of the Aldermanbury matrons who had been present when the midwife made her inspection, was then summoned and Dr Cox questioned her, after first asking Mrs Canning to leave the room. Mrs Woodward confirmed in every particular Mrs Canning's version of events: there had been 'soil upon the sleeves and neck', but 'freedom from stains on the lower parts'.

Dr Cox was back at Mr Marshall's house on Wednesday, 9th May. He again examined Elizabeth Canning, this time looking into her mouth for any scars – that would have been caused by mercury salivation – and whether there was any soreness or tendency for spitting.

Final examination was made the following Tuesday, now with the assistance of Mrs Oaks, senior midwife from the Lying-in Hospital in Brownlow Street. After she had examined the girl, Dr Cox himself inspected Elizabeth Canning's breasts and belly.

His conclusions were published in a best-selling pamphlet: *An appeal to the Public on behalf of Elizabeth Canning*. They fully confirmed those of James Solas Dodd. Dr Cox was convinced, on the basis of his extensive medical examinations, of the truth of Elizabeth Canning's story. Above all – like Henry Fielding – he was impressed by her 'fair character'. He was also convinced by the state of her shift on the night of 29th January; the irregularity of 'her courses' was entirely consistent with her taking cold at her washing ('it is no uncommon case with servants, who are obliged to dabble in cold water; the obstructions frequently continuing for some months, without any great complaints of illness'). Her costiveness added further credibility: 'as this state of the intestines was quite natural to her, and may be esteemed the principal natural course of the preservation of her life'.

Most importantly, Dr Cox could find no evidence that mercury had been administered by salivation for there were no scars in her mouth, neither was there any soreness. Furthermore, the blackish hue of her skin on 29th January, which was still retained on her arms on 30th March, was not consistent with what would be expected if there had been salivation for, in Dr Cox's view, mercury treatment would have left the skin 'fair and pale'.

As to the charge that Elizabeth Canning had given birth, Dr Cox was equally dismissive. Both he and Mrs Oaks, who had also consulted the Canning neighbours, Mrs Woodward and Mrs Rossiter, all declared their belief that 'Elizabeth Canning had never had a child'.

The remaining scandal – that she had been with a lover – was similarly discounted: 'One general reply may serve for all, let their truth be proved, and they will not fail gaining assent.'

Having delivered such decisive expert judgement, Dr Cox threw all caution to the winds and weighed in with as polemical a piece as was being produced in such profusion by the most ardent Canningites on their side of the battle.

The doctor had evidently been sleuthing on his own account. He relates how he met a Mr Hickman, distiller of Bishopgate Street, who said that at Mary Squires's and Mother Wells's trial he had heard the old gipsy woman say of Elizabeth Canning: 'Poor innocent creature, and so I did; I wish I had never seen her.' And there was the sworn statement of a Mr Mead, shoemaker of Silver Street, who had said he heard Mary Squires mutter to herself in Newgate Gaol, that Virtue Hall had turned her evidence to save Mother Wells and hang her – but that Mother Wells was as guilty as she. A Mr Surby – also of Silver Street – said much the same, according to Dr Cox, and that the old gipsy had expressed regret that 'the poor young gentlewoman [Elizabeth Canning] had been ill used'.

Another ostensibly medical pamphlet produced at the time (*The Imposture Detected; or, the Mystery and Iniquity of Elizabeth Canning's Story, Displayed; wherein Principles are laid down, and a method established, by which all impostures whatever, still prevailing in the world, may be detected; and all future ones for ever prevented from establishing themselves hereafter.*) took a very different line from those of Drs Dodd and Cox. The anonymous author opens by citing recent examples of metropolitan credulity: 'The rabbit-woman, the adventure of the quart-bottle, and the migration of the Londoners to the fields, occasioned by the soldiers prophesizing a third earthquake, are recent and notorious instances of this truth'.

The 'rabbit-woman' was purported to have given birth to a large number of rabbits. The 'quart-bottle' was a reference to the advertised claim that there would be a performance at the Haymarket Theatre in which all the instruments of the orchestra would be accurately reproduced by playing upon a walking stick. The performer would then disappear into a quart bottle, from where he would sing several songs while the bottle was handled by members of the audience. The performance would commence at half past six. A large audience assembled at the Haymarket and at seven o'clock, when the performer failed to materialise, set light to the stage and caused a great commotion in the street outside the theatre.

The absurd claims of Elizabeth Canning were just such an example of public credulity, the pamphlet maintained. How else was it possible to explain 'the obstinate, mountain-removing faith' of the Canningites? In the writer's opinion, Elizabeth Canning was herself a victim of her own delusions, had 'long been persuaded of the truth of her story' and was, consequently, 'not guilty of wilful perjury at the Old Bailey'. According to this view, 'her composed and uniform behaviour, before such tremendous men as the justice, and such fine men as the great lords and squires, that frequent the chocolate-houses, may likewise be accounted for'.

Contrary to Dr Dodd's diagnosis, the writer considered that Elizabeth Canning ('a hearty girl, sanguine, and of a florid countenance') would, on incarceration, have been quickly seized of one of 'Dr Boerhaare's first symptoms'; 'a strong canine appetite' with swift consumption of the dried bread, minced-pie and the pitcher of water. Another remarkable circumstance was the fact that the girl, being an epileptic, did not fall into a fit when Mary Squires cut off her stays.

In the writer's judgement, Elizabeth Canning was not a victim of syphilis – for which salivation might have been employed – 'because the virulence of this malady is prodigiously abated in comparison of what it was some years ago; that it is daily losing strength, and will in a short time entirely disappear'.

A more likely possibility, which would certainly account for the cessation of Elizabeth Canning's female benefit, was that she had had an abortion. 'What infamous means were used to bring about this infamous end, I cannot pretend to say . . . but be this as it will, it is certain, that an abortion at any rate, especially an artificial one, is always more dangerous, and attended with worse consequences, than even childbirth itself; so that it is no wonder she got back to her friends in such a piteous condition'.

*   *   *

The pamphleteers of 1753 were a mere advance guard for the legion that followed, which even included Voltaire, who later wrote a wildly inaccurate history of Elizabeth Canning. But in the May of that year appeared what was considered to be a most elegant piece; the one on which Voltaire largely based his history: *A letter to the right honourable the earl of ——— concerning the affair of Elizabeth Canning*, by 'a clergyman'.

The 'clergyman' was one of the most fashionable painters of his day; the favourite of George II – in the eyes of many, the superior of Joshua Reynolds and Gainsborough – with an independent fortune of more than forty thousand pounds. Allan Ramsay was a cultured man, a great traveller and an excellent linguist; a close friend of Dr Johnson. 'You will not find a man in whose conversation there is more instruction, more information and more elegance than Ramsay's', Johnson wrote.

Allan Ramsay returned to his native Edinburgh – after some years in London, the Grand Tour, studies at the French Academy and in Rome – but was staying in London in 1753. At forty this urbane, brown-eyed Scot, with his pugnacious jaw and attractively tilted nose, was keen to develop a reputation also as a writer. The Canning Affair gave him his chance: he penned his piece to the anonymous earl.

The 'letter', which extends to fifty-nine printed pages, starts with the polite hope that a previous one had been received – together with the tea and dimity [a cotton cloth] for her ladyship – and apologises for not having earlier communicated his opinions on the affair of Elizabeth Canning. It was only lately, the writer explains, that he had learned of the affair, of which he would most probably have remained in ignorance had it not been for the pamphlet of Mr Fielding, a gentleman for whom he has the highest regard. Ramsay could not, however, 'help being surprised to find upon what slight grounds he and many other sensible men, had founded their belief of her [Canning's] veracity'.

For Ramsay, it was a question of balancing an improbability against impossibility. Mr Fielding had ('very candidly') acknowledged the improbability of Elizabeth Canning's story, but had, nevertheless, convinced himself of its truth. Ramsay is forced to admit that 'the story of Canning is *possible*'. But then, 'so it would have been if she had gone a little farther and said she had been dead and buried during the time she was missing. For this is *possible*, and all that we could object to the relation of it is, that it is extremely *unusual* for dead people to return to life'.

After this shaky analogy, Allan Ramsay deploys a catechism of questions to show how *extremely* unusual was Miss Canning's account of her abduction.

Was it ever known that two footpads, after having committed a robbery for which they were both liable to be hanged, instead of flying from the watch, or *battering the skull of the robbed person with their clubs*, to prevent the appearance in judgement against them, ever made the robbed person a partner in their flight?

Was it ever known that two ruffians having committed a robbery, and as they had great reason to believe a murder, did ever persist in carrying or dragging the carcass of the murdered person ten miles, with much fatigue and hazard of being met; without its being possible for imagination to suggest any benefit, they could propose to themselves by this enterprise?

Was it ever read in any of the records of iniquity, that an old bawd and her associates were so ignorant of their own trade, as to think of winning a young girl to the ways of lewdness by hunger and cold, or to raise the price of her beauty by starving her black in the face?

And why, the painter demands, should so many people in the house remain silent on such a matter ('verging every hour towards murder') or remain patiently to be seized after their supposed guilt was discovered or, in the first place, have locked the girl in a room opening from a kitchen of a public bawdy house where her 'dying groan might have brought them all to the gallows?'

There were only two possible answers, Ramsay reasoned: 'either the circumstances are false, or that God Almighty has created a set of people at Enfield Wash, totally different in all their desires, fears, passions, and apprehensions, from the rest of mankind'.

And what happened to Elizabeth Canning on the road between Moorfields and Enfield, Ramsay wondered? By her account: 'NOTHING'. And in Mother Wells's kitchen? 'NEXT TO NOTHING'. Or during her twenty-eight days of confinement and the six hours she was on the road from Enfield to her mother's house? According to Miss Canning: 'NOTHING, NOTHING!'

Yet there are 'various ways of employing a month, besides

walking up and down in Mother Wells's hay-loft'. And Allan Ramsay thought it 'not amiss to hint' that 'there are such distempers as lyings-in and miscarriages, to which young servant-maids of eighteen are very much subject; distempers that will hold them as long, and reduce them as low as has been related of E. Canning, especially if attended and nursed in the manner we may easily suppose her to have been'. Furthermore, it would 'not be amiss to hint, that thirteen shillings and sixpence, with the sale of a gown and a pair of stays, is hardly more than sufficient to defray the expenses of such an operation; even altho' no part of it was expended in a christening, a wet nurse or a coffin, which, not to continue any idea of horror in your Lordship's imagination, might all have been provided by that most humane institution, the Foundling-Hospital'.

Piece by piece, Allan Ramsay examined every circumstance of the 'affair of Canning'. And each of them, he believed, carried 'the word LIE, in great letters upon its forehead'.

For Ramsay it was not merely an enquiry 'concerning a pair of old stays, or the bad diet of a servant wench; nor about the life of an old gipsy (tho' no man ought to think himself too great to interest himself in the distress of the meanest) but it is an enquiry of a much more interesting kind: *no less than an enquiry into the nature of moral evidence*, the axis upon which all human affairs turn'.

Dainty Davy and the Dorset Men

THE TRIALS OF the Abbotsbury men – on charges of 'wilful corrupt perjury' – had been set, at the July Sessions, for Thursday, 6th September, 1753, at the Old Bailey.

Sir Crisp Gascoyne had determined that, because of his hand in the Canning case, he should not preside at the trials. Accordingly, as the witnesses were called, he quit the chair, which was taken by Lord Chief Justice Willies: a clever old lecher who, it was widely believed, got his own maid-servants with child.

John Gibbons, William Clarke and Thomas Greville faced their trial, with – it was said – close on a hundred people on hand who had come up from Dorset and Wiltshire to testify on their behalf. Their lawyer was William Davy, the former Exeter grocer, who had defended Mary Squires and Susannah Wells in February. But there was no sign of Elizabeth Canning, or her lawyers, nor any of her witnesses, save for the solitary figure of Mary Woodward, Mrs Canning's neighbour from Aldermanbury Postern.

Then a man stepped forward bearing parchments. Who was he, demanded the court? And what were these documents? He was clerk to an attorney – a Mr Myles – came the reply. His master was out of town and he had been given the writs to deliver by Mr Myles's brother, the distiller; he himself knew nothing further of the matter.

The writs – requests for trial at the King's Bench – were a delaying tactic: the Canningites were determined that Elizabeth Canning should not come to the Old Bailey, nor that Gibbons, Clarke and Greville should have the chance of acquittal, while Crisp Gascoyne was Lord Mayor. To make doubly sure, they had sent Canning into hiding and kept the prosecution witnesses from court, except for Mrs Woodward and she only turned up because an officer went to fetch her.

Nevertheless, indictments were read, the first against John Gibbons and then against William Clarke and Thomas Greville (in that 'not having God before his eyes, but being moved and seduced by the instigation of the devil, and wickedly and unjustly devising and intending to pervert justice and to procure the said Mary Squires unjustly to be acquitted of the said crime laid to her charge').

All three were acquitted for lack of evidence against them, for still none of the prosecution witnesses appeared and Mary Woodward protested that she knew nothing of the matter. But in gaining his freedom Thomas Greville lost his life, for he caught smallpox in the court and was dead within the month.

The Canningites had, as they believed, protected Elizabeth from the prejudice of Sir Crisp Gascoyne – they had not known that he would withdraw – had prevented an embarrassing public recital of evidence by the Dorset and Wiltshire witnesses and foiled William Davy who was itching to cross-examine their heroine.

It was a typical Myles strategy, but not now engineered by John. He had found his client's supporters to be less than generous in paying his fees – and his considerable expenses – and had departed for Gloucestershire, taking all the legal documents with him. It was his brother, Thomas, the distiller, who had persuaded John Myles's clerk to appear at the Old Bailey bearing writs, with the story that his master was 'out of town'.

Meanwhile, the indictment against Elizabeth Canning remained. Yet despite innumerable writs – and warrant after warrant – she could not be found. But Crisp Gascoyne was determined to bring her to the Old Bailey, in the face of political unpopularity, the fury of the mob; mud thrown at his carriage and threats to his life.

Elizabeth Canning was publicly proclaimed an outlaw: in her parish church, on the hustings at Guildhall and in the Quarter Sessions. In November the new Lord Mayor was installed, but still there was no sign of Miss Canning. Public interest began to wane; the torrent of pamphlets and cartoons slowed to a trickle. Then at the February Sessions of 1754, as her outlawry was about to be again proclaimed, Elizabeth Canning reappeared at the Old Bailey and offered herself for trial.

*   *   *

On Monday 29th April, 1754, Elizabeth Canning was brought to the bar at Justice Hall in the Old Bailey to face trial – like the Abbotsbury men – for wilful and corrupt perjury ('in unlawfully, wickedly, maliciously, and deliberately advising, contriving, and intending to pervert the due course of law and justice, and to procure the said Mary Squires untruly to be convicted of felony and robbery').

Justice Hall was jammed to the doors that spring morning. Spectators jostled and fought – risking gaol-fever and smallpox – while fine ladies peered down from the balcony to glimpse the scullery-maid who was once more the talk of London.

Elizabeth Canning stood, demure and impassive, at the centre of the packed courtroom, before Thomas Rawlinson – the new Lord Mayor – and His Majesty's other Justices of Oyer and Terminer, while the Clerk of Arraigns ploughed through endless legal rigmarole.

Three of the black-gowned lawyers – lounging and yawning, in their twin-tailed wigs, at the table before the bar – were linked by more than chance circumstance. William Davy had

again been set against Elizabeth Canning and was determined
– this time – to bring her down. At his side was Bamber
Gascoyne – Sir Crisp's eldest son – and Edward Willies, son of
the lecherous Lord Chief Justice Willies, who had presided at
the trials of the Abbotsbury men after Sir Crisp had quit the
chair.

Bamber Gascoyne opened quietly for the prosecution with a
brief, sober account of Elizabeth Canning's supposed ordeal in
January of the year before. William Davy followed, waxing
eloquent – probing every improbability and inconsistency –
preparing the ground for Edward Willies to launch forth in
vigorous style.

'Gentlemen, the prisoner stands indicted of one of the most
heinous crimes; an endeavour, by wilful and corrupt fore-
swearing herself, to take away the life of a guiltless person;
and with aggravation, in the black catalogue of offences, I
know not one of a deeper dye. It is a perversion of the laws of
her country to the worst of purposes; it is wrestling the sword
out of the hands of justice to shed innocent blood.'

Mr Willies could only thank God and King George for the
mercy that had been shown to Mary Squires, for certainly
Elizabeth Canning's 'cruel heart' had never relented.

'When I think of the age of the prisoner at the bar, scarcely
yet above nineteen-years-old, I can hardly persuade myself
that human nature could so early attain to such a pitch of
wickedness: but when I attend to the very strong and
convincing proofs we have to produce against her, I must give
up my reason to my incredulity, if I any longer doubted,
whether she was guilty or not'.

*   *   *

The prosecution's first task was to prove the alibis of Mary
Squires: that she had been in Dorset, with George and Lucy, in
January when Elizabeth Canning had sworn that she had cut
off her stays and locked her in the loft at Enfield Wash.

The old gipsy had arrived in some style at the Old Bailey,

87

with two men carrying her in a chair, George and Lucy at her side. She was wearing a black bonnet, with a white napkin pinned beneath it, and a white shawl. Yet she looked weak and her head was wobbling.

George Squires cut a smart figure, with a decent bluish suit and a brown bob-wig: which was more than could be said of his performance as a witness when William Davy tried to establish the Squires's whereabouts before Christmas of 1752.

'What was the last village you came from when you came to South Perrott?'

'I cannot recollect it,' George replied.

'Where did you lie the night before you came to South Perrott?'

'I cannot tell the place's name,' came the reply.

Mr Davy tried again, like a sheepdog trying to drive a particularly stupid charge into the fold.

'How long had your mother, sister, and you been travelling together?'

'I came home from Newington Butts in Southwark, and I went from thence – as near as I can guess – about seven or eight weeks before Michaelmas.'

'Can't you recollect the place you lay at before you came to South Perrott?' Davy demanded, with increasing irritation – and complete lack of success.

Slowly and painfully, William Davy led the gipsy across Dorset, retracing the steps he said he had taken with his old mother and Lucy: from Litton Cheyney to Abbotsbury – and the New Year's festivities – to Portesham; then on to Ridgeway – where the dead horse was skinned – and half across England to Mother Wells's house at Enfield Wash.

William Davy paused and pointed at Elizabeth Canning. 'Did you see this young woman at the bar when you were there?'

'No, I did not. I never saw her before we were taken up in my life. If I was to be racked to death, I'll stand with a sword put to my heart if I ever saw her till she came in the chaise.'

George Squires's bluster was soon deflated by Elizabeth Canning's counsel, Mr Morton, who pressed him closely, battering him with questions on the geography of the home counties.

'I had not thought of being called to such questions as these,' George protested.

'I shall ask you a great many questions you have not heard yet,' threatened Morton, resuming his onslaught. 'After you left Lewes, what is the first town that you came to that you did know?'

'Really I do not know,' George stuttered. 'It is so long ago, I can't tell you.'

'You, without an almanack, have given a long and seeming fair account of a long journey,' Morton persisted. 'Pray trace yourself down into Dorsetshire; I don't ask you the first town from Lewes, but the first town you do remember *after* you left Lewes.'

George Squires made no reply.

'It was not South Perrott, was it?'

'No, it is not possible I can tell you. I went from thence into Hampshire and Wiltshire; I went through Salisbury.'

Steadily, Elizabeth Canning's counsel harried the gipsy. Could he name any town he passed through between Lewes and Salisbury? In what country is Salisbury? What was the next town when he left Mere? Did he lie in Lewes? Name one great town after Shaftesbury. What was the *exact* time he set out from Newington Butts? What time did his mother get back to Litton from Abbotsbury? Was he positive it *was* in the year 1752 that he made his journey?

Eventually, Mr Morton finished his catechism and the court waited expectantly for the next witness: Lucy Squires. But William Davy had changed his mind.

'We will not call the sister,' he announced. 'She is rather more stupid than her brother, and has not been on the road since their coming to Enfield Wash.'

Mr Davy had in mind someone who *had* been on the road with George Squires: an agent of Sir Crisp Gascoyne who could 'assign the reason of this man's [Squires] remembering the times and places of their return from the west with such exactness, when he can recollect so little of his journey going down'.

But Mr Morton would have none of this. It could only be hearsay, he claimed. And the court agreed.

So, Sir Crisp's man did not appear, Lucy did not give her evidence and a chastened George went back to sit between his sister and his mother in her armchair.

The men from Litton Cheyney were the next to step up: the tiler, who testified that he saw the gipsies walk into the village on Saturday, 30th December, and then Francis Gladman and James Angel and John Hawkins, the publican, who swore much the same. They were all entirely clear as to the date because of the ringing-in of the New Year by the church bells on the Monday.

Then came the Abbotsbury men.

Lucy's suitor told how George Squires had called at his house on New Year's Eve and how, on the following day, they had walked back together to Litton Cheyney. Clarke was closely questioned about his dinner that day.

'Do you remember anything of a couple of fowls?' Mr Gascoyne enquired.

'We eat something there,' Clarke replied. 'I took part of a fowl.'

'Was it roast or boiled?'

'It was boiled fowl, to the best of my remembrance.'

Mr Williams – Elizabeth Canning's Junior Counsel – was also interested in Clarke's dinner on New Year's day, 1753.

'What time did Mary Squires come in after you were in Litton?'

'She might come in in half an hour, and that might be between three and four o'clock. We took part of a fowl there.'

'What amongst you all?'

'Yes, amongst us all,' Clarke replied.

'Was it boiled or roasted?'

'To the best of my remembrance, it was boiled.'

'Who paid the reckoning?'

'I don't know indeed, I did not pay a farthing.'

This was awkward: William Clarke had said they had shared *part* of a fowl; George Squires, in his evidence, that they ate *two* whole birds. William Davy jumped up to mend the breach.

'When you came to Litton, had Lucy and Mary Squires sat down to dinner?'

'No, Sir,' replied Clarke.

'Did you see the dish when first served up?'

'I eat part of what was meddled with.'

'Had they been eating before you came there?'

'I don't know whether they had eat anything or not.'

That was good enough. Clarke had evidently not noticed what he was eating, Lucy must have been a distraction.

Clarke was then questioned about the celebrations on the evening of New Year's Day, 1753; as was the landlord and the other Abbotsbury men.

John Ford, the carpenter, was cross-examined by Mr Morton about his remembrance of the gipsies' arrival.

'How early on the Monday did you see them there?'

'It was some time about one, two, or three o'clock; I am sure it was sometime in the afternoon. I know it was not night, because I was looking over the hatch, and saw George coming down the street, and spoke to him.'

'How far might you see George, before he came to speak to you?'

'I saw him, perhaps, fifty yards – I could see a hundred – and I believe I could see a thousand yards,' said Ford expansively.

'What hour do you take it to be?' Morton enquired.

'I am sure it was not come to three o'clock; upon my life I kissed Lucy before three o'clock.'

Ford had held his own about the time of the gipsies' arrival at Abbotsbury, despite an awkward discrepancy between his and George Squires's and William Clarke's evidence. The carpenter had said they had arrived at Abbotsbury *before* three o'clock, whereas the other two claimed that they did not leave Litton Cheyney until well after this time. William Davy was on his feet to repair the damage.

'You say the first time you saw them was on Monday the 1st of January. Pray what time of day was that?'

'I went to the ale house between one and two o'clock for a mug of beer,' Ford retorted.

'How many pots of beer have you drunk today?' Davy sneered. 'Do you take upon you to say you saw them on the Monday about two or three in the afternoon?'

'I did,' said Ford defiantly.

'You are drunk now', Davy retorted, 'and ought to be ashamed of yourself.'

There was no such trouble with the next witness when he was examined by Mr Gascoyne. Andrew Wake had documentary evidence: his journal, which showed that he arrived at The Ship at Abbotsbury on 31st December, 1752.

'Look at the old woman sitting there, do you know her?' Gascoyne asked.

'I do, it is Mary Squires', came the reply. 'I saw her at Abbotsbury, at Gibbons's house, at that time, the 31st of December.'

Wake also recognised George (whom he could have seen on the 31st; although his mother was said not to have arrived until the following day). He first met the gipsy at The Ship ('sitting by the kitchen fire'). He had read about 'this affair of the trial of the old woman' in the newspapers and was eventually called to attend upon the Lord Mayor who sent him on to Newgate to identify Mary Squires.

'Did Mary Squires recollect you?' asked Mr Williams during cross-examination.

'I said nothing at all to her, only asked her if she knew me. She said "Yes". That I was the young man belonging to the excise office. And she said she remembered me very well, that I borrowed her son's greatcoat.'

'Did she seem to be under any hesitation at the time?'

'No, she seemed to be rather overjoyed; she knew me through the grate as she was in the press yard.'

Other Dorset witnesses were equally confident that they had seen the gipsies in the cold wet days of early January, 1753.

The Abbotsbury schoolmaster had good reason to remember them. On the evening of Monday, 8th January, he had returned tired from Devonshire – where he had been visiting his sick wife – to find that the exciseman had been given his bed at The Old Ship and that George Squires was also sleeping in the room.

'When I came home, my landlady begged I would not be offended at her putting somebody in my bed – that was this exciseman. There are two beds in the room, and in the other George Squires lay.'

'What time did you see this old woman on the 8th?' Mr Morton asked, pointing to Mary Squires.

'It was after candles were lighted,' the schoolmaster explained. 'After I had shifted myself, I came and sat down by the fire, with George Squires and Mr Wake. I had never seen George before. I asked my landlady who he was. She said his name was Squires, and that his mother and sister were in another room; after which the old woman came out to call her son to go to bed.'

The next day, the master said he was standing in the street – at the school door – drinking a mug of beer, when George Squires and William Clarke came by.

'What might it be o'clock?' Mr Morton asked.

'It might be five o'clock; I saw no more of him. George said he would not stay any longer, for he must go to Portesham. I did not go out, but went to bed afterwards.'

The gipsies' move to Portesham was confirmed by the village tailor. His son, John, was equally certain that he had seen the gipsies in Abbotsbury. He could be particular as to the date, because he had gone to Abbotsbury on Epiphany Day, 6th January, and had noticed them there.

The landlord of The Sloop Aground, and the Abbotsbury

man who had been selling turnips, also remembered seeing the gipsies at Ridgeway, on the day the horse was being skinned. John Taylor of Fordington said that he watched them, later, crossing the swollen ford on 11th January.

Step by step, Messrs Davy, Gascoyne and Willies paraded their witnesses, moving from Chettle to Martin and then across the Wiltshire border to Coombe, where Thomas Greville's widow testified, as also did half a dozen others, that the 'old woman, the girl in the Capuchin hood and the man behind her' – Mrs Greville pointed to them in court – had stayed the night of the 14th at The Lamb.

Another witness swore that the gipsies had been in Basingstoke and that she had written the letter for Lucy to her young man. Two more testified that they were in Brentford, on the 22nd and 23rd; another couple that the Squires arrived in Tottenham on 23rd January.

It was an impressive achievement for the prosecution. Forty-one people had positively sworn that Mary Squires had been travelling, with George and Lucy, from the Somerset border to Middlesex at the time that Elizabeth Canning had testified – and practically all of London had believed that they had been at Enfield Wash. It had taken an entire day in the packed Justice Hall for William Davy, Bamber Gascoyne and Edward Willies to bring the three gipsies from South Perrott to within three miles of Mother Wells's house. The city clocks were clanging ten o'clock, on that spring night in 1754, when William Davy finally sat down at the long lawyers' table in the Old Bailey. Outside, the crowd – which had expected a verdict that night – was waiting to cheer their chaste heroine home and abuse anyone who dared speak against her. A great howl went up when Sir Crisp Gascoyne appeared in the street. The mob surged forward. Dirt and stones flew; women cursed the monster who had forced an innocent maid to unjust trial. Sir Crisp's friends closed around and hurried him to safety in a nearby tavern. Balked, the mob rampaged after the old gipsy. Failing to find her – and after breaking more windows – the crowd remembered their original intent and headed back to escort the object of their devotion, hanging on to the side of her coach as it inched its way along the Old Bailey, fighting to catch a glimpse of the Aldermanbury scullery-maid.

12

Not One Tittle of Hay

IT WAS AN historic decision to adjourn the trial of Elizabeth Canning. Then, it was not customary for a court to rise until a verdict was returned. But Thomas Rawlinson was in an impossible position, for William Davy had produced such a parade of witnesses as was never seen before in an English court and – at ten o'clock that night – still had more to come. Furthermore, as the new Lord Mayor was aware, the verdict in the Elizabeth Canning case would have explosive consequences – whichever way it went. It was essential, therefore, that all the evidence should be heard, and be seen to be examined with the utmost thoroughness with the court in a proper physical and mental state so to do.

An eighteenth century scullery-maid thus produced an unexpected and lasting benefit for English Law by establishing the important principle that, in cases of misdemeanour, the court may adjourn and the jury separate. However, it was not until forty years later that it was determined that a jury may retire to bed before producing a verdict in cases of felony and treason.

The trial of Elizabeth Canning was, in fact, adjourned for two whole days because several of the aldermen on the bench were standing in the Parliamentary election on the Tuesday.

Although Sir Crisp Gascoyne had hoped to enter Parliament for Southwark after his mayoralty, he was bottom of the poll: the Canning affair had made him the most unpopular man in London.

The behaviour of the mob became an issue in the propaganda war between Canningites and Egyptians.

On 1st May, the *Daily Advertiser*, which was an anti-Canningite journal, carried the following paragraph:

This Morning at Nine o'clock will be continued the Trial of Elizabeth Canning. At the breaking up of the Court on Monday Night a Mob (as it may reasonably be believed) hired for the Purpose, were Guilty of many Insults and Abuses on the Persons who appeared on behalf of the Prosecution; the Evidence for which, we are credibly informed, are threatened with Destruction. Must it not appear an extraordinary instance of the Girl's Innocence, that those who have so long endeavoured to elude the Court of Justice, by a continued train of Artifice, now seek to impede it by Violence and Outrage.

The Canningite reply was on the streets that very afternoon: a handbill addressed to the multitude that still thronged outside the Old Bailey.

To the Persons assembled about the *Sessions House*
in the *Old Bailey*.

Wednesday, May 1

Although nothing can be said to have been proved against Elizabeth Canning till her Evidence has been heard, which before Tomorrow Night may establish her Innocence beyond a Doubt; yet various Attempts have been made to prejudice the Public against her. Among other Charges utterly false and infamous, it has been published, that her Managers (who have scarcely received enough from the charitably disposed to pay the current Charge of this tedious

Trial) have hired you to obstruct Justice. None of you present, none living, can say, that one Word prompting you to espouse her Side has been uttered by any one concerned for her. If you have any Regard for Publick Justice, for this poor injured Girl, or for yourselves – by all that is dear to you, be persuaded to Peace, and without the least Murmur or Insult to say, to wait the Event of this Business – God and her Innocence have hitherto supported her, in the Opinion of many thro' unexampled Distresses: Leave it to God and her Innocence only to carry her through this, and all will be well.

*　　*　　*

The second day of Elizabeth Canning's trial opened with a harrowing account, by the Recorder, of the attack on Sir Crisp Gascoyne, and of the insults to which the jury had been exposed by the 'insolence of a mob', on the Monday night. It was moved, and granted, that 'a sufficient guard' should be provided both for Sir Crisp and the members of the jury.

After apologies from Elizabeth Canning's counsel (for the 'misguided zeal of the multitude' which 'ought not to be imputed to her or her friends') and some sparring about the 'cruel, unjust and illegal' paragraph in the *Daily Advertiser* (which had attributed the violence of the mob to the 'persons who appeared on behalf of the prosecution') William Davy rose to announce that his first witness was Alderman Chitty: the only snag being that the alderman was not in court.

Mr Chitty hurried in as the next witness was being sworn, but was quickly brought forward to be examined by Bamber Gascoyne.

'Be pleased, Sir, to give an account of what passed before you on 31st of January 1753, relating to Elizabeth Canning.'

'I was the sitting alderman at that time. Elizabeth Canning was brought before me, but as it is about a year and a half ago, I cannot give a distinct account of it. I remember it was on the 31st January, about half an hour after twelve, or one o'clock.

The Trial of Elizabeth Canning

Mr Lyon or another person – I believe it was Mr Nash – came to me. There are a few notes taken for my own memorandum, which I believe are in court, which are the substance of what passed.'

Alderman Chitty began to read. How Elizabeth Canning had come to him at the Justice Room, in the Guildhall, on 31st January 1753. That she had sworn that on New Year's Day as she was returning from her uncle's house, she had been set upon, at near ten o'clock, by two men who stripped and robbed her of half-a-guinea, three shillings and a halfpenny.

'Are you sure she said a halfpenny?' William Davy butted in.

99

'I am sure she did, also her gown from her back.'

The alderman ploughed on, about how she had struggled – as a handkerchief was stuffed into her mouth – and was stunned by a blow on the head. How she was forced along Bishopgate Street ('each holding her up under her arms'), but did not remember anything more until about half an hour before they arrived – as she later learned – at Mother Wells's house. How there were several persons in the room to which she was taken. And they had said 'she must do as they did, and if so, she should have fine clothes, etc.' When she refused, 'a woman forced her up stairs into a room, and, with a case-knife she had in her hand, cut the lace of her stays, and took her stays away, and told her there was bread and water in the said room, and if she made any noise she would come in immediately and cut her throat.' In the room in which she was imprisoned was 'an old stool or two, an old table, and an old picture over the chimney, two windows in the room, one fastened up with boards, the other part ditto and part glass, in which latter she made a hole by removing a pane, and forced part open, and got out on a small shed of boards or penthouse, and so slid down and jumped down on the side of a bank on the backside of the house.'

'During the time of this examination, did she mention any hay?' Bamber Gascoyne enquired.

'She said there was nothing in the room but those things she had mentioned; not one tittle of hay, neither do I remember what she said she lay upon.'

'Did she describe any gipsy, or any remarkable woman?'

'I asked her, whether she should know the woman again? She said, she believed she should; but she did not make mention of any extraordinary woman doing this.'

When Bamber Gascoyne had finished with Alderman Chitty, William Davy rose to take his turn: questioning Gawen Nash, the coffee-house keeper of Gutter Lane.

Nash had been among the fifty or so people who had packed into the Justice Room at the Guildhall, when Alderman Chitty made out his warrant for the arrest of Mother Wells. He had gone ('cheek-by-jowl') with Edward Lyon – after his friend had paid the shilling for the warrant – they ('being very intimate') had returned to his house with the intention of setting off for Enfield Wash that very afternoon. But Mrs Nash was firmly opposed to her husband spending a night out of town. So it was agreed that they should set off next morning by coach with two other friends: Messrs Aldridge and Hague.

It was 'all in uproar' when they had arrived at Mother Wells's.

Only the loft ('a nasty room') remotely resembled the one in which Elizabeth Canning said she was locked. Yet Mr Nash could not even see a key-hole in the door; neither were there any signs of where a lock or a bolt could have been attached. And it was a very long room. When he came down from the loft he spoke to Mr White (the Lord Mayor's Marshal-man).

'I said to him, "For God's sake, what do you think of this affair?"' Mr Nash recalled. 'He said, he believed we were got into the wrong box, and he said, he believed the girl had never been there.'

All this was going on before Elizabeth Canning arrived, Mr Nash explained. When they went back to the loft, he voiced his doubts again – for the girl had said that it had been an empty, dark room. But Mr Lyon had argued that 'these things may have been put here since'.

Patiently, William Davy extracted every detail of the loft at Mother Wells's house. Were there cobwebs on the casement? Was there dust in the hearth? Were there any signs of pictures having been over the chimney? How far from the window was the ground? Were there any trees in the hedge near the window? What part of the room did the hay lay in?

Next, Gawen Nash described Elizabeth Canning's arrival at Enfield Wash. How the girl was brought in and set on the dresser – from which she could have seen up into the loft through its open door – and then on a broken stool, with her back to the fire, from which she could see the dresser and, still, the stairs leading up to the loft.

When Elizabeth Canning was carried into the parlour, Mary Squires was sitting upon a low chair, on the right-hand side of the fireplace. She was wearing a black bonnet and, according to Gawen Nash, almost doubled up. He could not see her face. But Elizabeth Canning pointed immediately to Mary Squires and said, 'That old woman in the corner was the woman that robbed me.'

Nash's companions, John Hague and Edward Aldridge, the silversmith, told virtually the same story. Neither of them had been able to see the old gipsy's face when Elizabeth Canning had pointed to her. Both of them had noticed the hole in the wall of the loft through which the jack line passed and which, according to Hague, was large enough for a cat to go through and for Elizabeth Canning to have spotted a mouse in the other room. Hague had been convinced by Virtue Hall's denial, that she had never seen Elizabeth Canning at Mother Wells's and had been sickened by her testimony at Mary Squires's trial when he was convinced that she was perjuring herself.

Edward Aldridge said he was so disillusioned by the goings-on at Mother Wells's house that he went to an ale house – for mutton chops and half a pint of wine – rather than go on to Mr Justice Tyshmaker's with the others.

It was very odd, Elizabeth Canning's counsel thought, that Mr Aldridge should have disbelieved his client's evidence. If he had, then why did he call on a neighbour of Mrs Wells – taking with him a relative of his from Enfield Wash, also called Edward Aldridge – to collect money for a fund for Elizabeth Canning?

'I was going down to Enfield Wash, I cannot tell how long after,' Aldridge babbled. 'I don't know whether it was not that week. I hardly knew the gentleman; I have heard say he is a surveyor of the window lights. I remember I went down to Mr Edward Aldridge's at Enfield Wash. When I went out, I was desired to take some of the papers – her printed case in order for a subscription – to Mr Aldridge there.'

'I'll put you in mind of one thing: did you or did you not, say you were satisfied with the girl's description she gave of the house, either to Mr or Mrs Howard?'

'I denied it from the very first.'

But the silversmith admitted that there had been talk of the old gipsy – and how long she had been there – and that it had been a full month after she was convicted, before he went to the Lord Mayor and then only under the strong persuasion of Mr Nash and Mr Hague.

'Did you not think it a matter of justice to go?' Mr Williams demanded.

'When I was called for, I did: it was no business of mine to trouble my head about it to go.'

After the Lord Mayor's Marshal-man – whose evidence tallied in all important respects with those of the three preceding witnesses – came the Natuses: first Fortune and then Judith.

He described the loft in exact detail ('a long room, no squareness belongs to it, with a pantile roof') together with every item that had cluttered the place in which he swore he had slept with his wife since 'the Monday fortnight after my Lord Mayor's day, of Sir Crisp Gascoyne's mayoralty' (November, 1752). It was he who had put a wisp of hay in the hole in the wall, to keep out the cold. He had *never* in all his life seen Elizabeth Canning until he had been called from his work to go to Mr Tyshmaker's house. Furthermore, he (Natus) swore that several persons – including a man in search of the irons for an inn sign and people taking pollard to feed Mother Wells's sow – had gone into the loft. Under cross-examination, Fortune Natus maintained that he 'never knew any harm by the house'. Although 'the people that belong to the house have got a very bad character' he 'never saw any harm in it' for it was 'a very sober, honest house' in which he 'never saw any ill tricks or irregularity' all the time he was there.

Judith Natus said much the same, providing yet another inventory of the contents of her threadbare home, with its pile of hay for a bed and the chest of drawers in which she kept her bread and cheese, so that the mice should not run away with it. Mrs Natus swore that she had never seen the bedgown, or the handkerchief, which William Davy held out for her inspection.

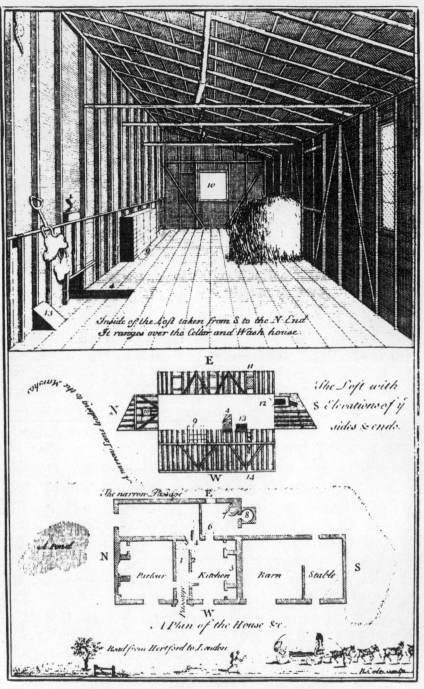

Inside of the Loft taken from S to the N End
It ranges over the Cellar and Wash house.

The Loft with
Elevations of ye
sides & ends.

A narrow Lane leading to the Marshes

The narrow Passage

N   S

Parlour   Kitchen   Barn   Stable

A Plan of the House &c

Road from Hertford to London

A Plan of Susannah Wells's House at Enfield Wash and a
Perspective View of Eliz. Canning's supposed Prison

She had certainly never set eyes on Elizabeth Canning until she came with the others to carry them before Mr Justice Tyshmaker.

Mrs Natus was the last witness to give evidence that day.

Outside, the crowd was in even more vicious mood, inflamed rather than passified by the Canningite handbills that had been distributed in the afternoon, and which served only to remind them further of the injuries, distress and wrongs to their innocent maid. Such was the fury of the mob, that the Lord Mayor read the Riot Act that night outside the Old Bailey on May Day, 1754.

13

The Canningites Rally

THE JUSTICE HALL at the Old Bailey lay silent the following morning. There was more polling to be done. Five aldermen on the bench, who were candidates, wanted to keep an eye on things, so the court was adjourned again. After his defeat at Southwark, Sir Crisp Gascoyne did not go to the poll that day.

William Davy resumed his parade of witnesses on the following Friday morning.

The chandler's wife from Enfield Wash, said she knew Fortune Natus and his wife very well – they dealt with her for groceries – and she often saw them, from Michaelmas until the day Mother Wells and Mary Squires were taken up. She never saw the gipsies there before Wednesday, 24th January. They came for bread, cheese and small beer – on that very day – and then almost daily to her shop. She put the coins she took from the old gipsy into a pail of water, because she had heard they could get back the money again.

Elizabeth Canning's counsel was intrigued.

'Whose money were you afraid would be so nimble, Lucy's or the old woman's?'

'I had put Lucy's in my pocket amongst the other money. It was the old woman's money I put in the water.'

Sarah Howit, Mrs Wells's daughter, said she slept at her mother's house all through December and January. She and Virtue Hall were often in the loft fetching pollard for the sow. They were up there – leaning out of the window – on the 8th January, when three local lads came to lop one of the trees, whose branches came to within a couple of yards of the house. One of them, a costermonger, had thrown dirt up at the window. 'Don't, you'll break the windows,' Sal had called out as the two girls came to the window when 'Virtue Hall looked under Sal's breast, and Sal stood over the shoulder of Virtue Hall'. The costermonger had climbed the tree ('just against the window') that afternoon and larked with the two girls for upwards of ten minutes. There was no sign of Elizabeth Canning in the loft. Afterwards, the men said they drank beer that Mother Wells paid for: the truth of which Mr Cantril, the publican, was in court to testify; as was Ezra Whiffin the landlord of The White Hart and Crown, who recounted his visit to Susannah Wells's loft, on the 18th January, in search of the iron work for an inn sign, for which he paid one shilling, disturbing Judith Natus – on her bed of hay – in the process. His son, John, confirmed his evidence. He was the fiftieth witness to be brought forward by William Davy.

And still they came on: Mrs Wells's daughter, Elizabeth Long, and her son, John Howit; then a man who had played cards with Fortune and Judith Natus during both Old and New Christmases of the year before. A carpenter and surveyor produced plans, elevations, perspective views and, finally, a wooden scale model of Mother Wells's ramshackle loft.

Mrs Mayle, the midwife, gave, yet again, her opinion that Elizabeth could not have been debauched, there being no stains from copulation on the shift and only three spots of excrement. She was convinced that the garment could not have been worn above a week.

'What was your reason for being so inquisitive in this?' asked Mr Williams.

'I was so, as a lover of truth – and a friend – fearing the girl had been debauched', was the confident reply.

After the midwife, came Henry Fielding's clerk. He had been hauled up to testify to the information which Elizabeth Canning had given to his master, on 7th February, 1753, and to sift through it so that the court could register every word.

Then came Mr Deputy Molineux. He had been with Sir Crisp Gascoyne when Elizabeth Canning and Virtue Hall were brought to the Mansion House for examination and the famous bedgown was handed round. Mr Molineux swore that he heard Elizabeth Canning say (in reply to the Lord Mayor's command, 'You must not take it away'): 'Yes, my Lord, I must – it is my *mother's.*'

Samuel Reed swore the same. 'I was present the time Mr Molineux speaks of. I very particularly remember she was going to fold up this bedgown. My Lord Mayor said, "Child, you must not have that." She said, "It is my mother's", which struck me very much.'

Mr Reed was the last of the sixty witnesses William Davy marshalled to bring down Elizabeth Canning.

*   *   *

The defence opened after dinner, but it was evening before Mr Nares and Mr Morton finished their speeches and Mr Williams rose to examine the kindly old carpenter to the Goldsmith's Company, who had known Elizabeth Canning from childhood, and for whose wife she had scrubbed and washed in Aldermanbury Postern.

Edward Lyon explained that – 'being thick of hearing' – he could not give much account of what passed before Alderman Chitty when the warrant was granted. He also seems to have been hard pushed to follow events at Enfield Wash – when they all rode out with Mr White, the Marshal-man – for the place had been so full of people. But he believed that Elizabeth Canning had seen the old gipsy's face 'before she fixed upon her person'.

'Why do you think so?' asked Mr Williams.

'I think she would hardly charge her without sight of her face; I have no other reason.'

'When Mary Squires was charged with being the person, what was done?'

'She came up to her, and said, I hope you will not swear my life away, for I never saw you. Then Betty Canning was carried into the kitchen.'

'Did you hear Mary Squires say where she was at the time?'

'I did not hear anything of that.'

'Did you hear Elizabeth Canning, or anybody else, say what day the robbery was committed?'

'No, I did not hear anybody say anything of it.'

Had he ever heard Mr Nash or Mr Aldridge say that they did not believe a word of Elizabeth Canning's story?

'No, not at all, upon no account.'

'Did you ever hear Mr Aldridge say so?'

'No. Mr Aldridge I have seen casually pass and repass – "Your humble servant," and so on – but I was not in his company. When I saw Mr Nash on the morning of the trial of the gipsy it was "Your servant," and so on; but no conversation.'

The treachery of Gawen Nash and Edward Aldridge was revealed in a note, from Nash to Mr Lyon written on 10th February, 1753, which was read to the court ['I am informed by Mr Aldridge, who has been at Enfield, that if a person be appointed there to receive contributions, some money would be raised in that place for the unhappy poor girl.']

Thomas Colley was cross-examined in detail about Elizabeth Canning's diet during her visit to his home on New Year's Day, 1753. The prosecution was, evidently, anxious to establish to what extent it would have sustained her through twenty-eight days of virtual starvation.

'Did she eat a hearty dinner?' Edward Willies enquired.

What was she given to drink – it being New Year's Day? Did Mrs Colley generally have bread and butter or toast with her tea? How much of the sirloin had the girl eaten that night? How much drink after that? Did the Colleys have mince-pies in the house? Where might she have come by a penny-pie?

Elizabeth Canning's counsel could bear it no longer.

'Was the toast buttered on *both* sides, do you think?' he burst out, in sarcastic exasperation. 'Here have been a great many questions asked in order to force a stool.'

'I cannot tell,' the bewildered glass-blower replied.

Mr Morton's interjection achieved modest immortality. The comedian, Samuel Foote, incorporated it in one of his farces in which he brought the house down nightly by very successfully mimicking Edward Willies's mannerisms, but using Morton's words.

Alice Colley was the last witness in the Sessions House that night. She told how she and her husband had walked back with her niece ('on New Year's day a twelve month') as far as the corner of Houndsditch and had leaned on a post as they watched her walk away.

A huge crowd was waiting outside the Old Bailey. But the reading of the Riot Act on the previous night, and the hauling up of three of the mob to make proper submission to the court, seemed to have done the trick, for there were no brickbats or invective that night as Bet Canning was again cheered all the way to her lodgings.

*   *   *

The next morning – the fourth of the trial – Elizabeth's mother was examined and cross-examined. William Davy pressed her hard about her daughter's disappearance and the efforts which she had made to look for her. The flustered widow protested that she 'went to all the agents and places' that she could think of 'fearing some casualty'.

'Did you go to a conjuror?'

'I did. They called him the astrologer.'

'Where does he live?' Davy demanded.

'He lives in the Old Bailey.'

'What is his name?'

'I don't know his name. He had a black wig over his face.'

'When did you go to him?'

'I don't know when I went.'

'How long after your daughter was missing?'

'It was before she returned.'

'What was done there?'

'I told him I had lost my child; and after he had got my money he bid me go home and advertise her. He said, "Make yourself easy, she'll come home again."'

'Did he tell you when she should return?'

'No he did not,' Mrs Canning retorted. 'He only asked me two or three questions, and wrote, scribble, scribble, scribble along.'

'Did he tell you she was in the hands of an old woman?'

'No, he did not.'

'Recollect yourself,' William Davy admonished.

'I don't know whether he did or no: he might for what I know.'

'Or what misfortune had happened to her?'

'No.'

'Whether he did not tell you she was in the hands of an old black woman?'

'The word "black" I don't remember. I know he frightened me. When he shut the door, and lighted the candles up, he looked so frightful, I was glad to get out of the door again.'

Relentlessly, Davy pursued the matter of Mrs Canning's visit to the Old Bailey conjuror – trying to show that she had known more than she admitted – before turning to her daughter's return to Aldermanbury Postern.

'How did she look when she came home?'

'Her face was swelled, bloated, and black, and sodden, as if it had lain in water, and her arms black. She swallowed nothing hardly.'

Mr Davy was interested to find out about Robert Scarrat – the journeyman hartshorn-scraper – who so immediately brought up the name of Mother Wells when Elizabeth Canning said she spotted, from her prison, the coachman who had driven her mistress into Hertfordshire.

'Did he tell you that he had formerly been at Mother Wells's?'

'No, never,' the widow replied.

'Did you never hear him say he had jumped out of the window himself?'

'No, I never did.'

Robert Scarrat faced Mr Davy, after James Lord, the apprentice, had sworn that he was positive that his mistress had not known of her daughter's whereabouts on New Year's Day the year before.

Scarrat admitted that he had visited Mother Wells's house when he worked for Mr Snee of Edmonton.

'How often have you been at the house of Mother Wells?' William Davy demanded.

'I have once or twice.'

'Will you venture to swear that you have not been there oftener than twice?'

'I may have been there two or three times.'

'Have you been there no more than three times, upon your oath?'

'I cannot say whether I have or have not,' Scarrat spluttered. 'I have called, maybe three or four times. I don't know.'

'Upon your oath, you have not been there five times?'

'I don't know. I cannot say how many times.'

'Will you take it upon you to say, you have not been there six times?'

'No!'

'Upon your oath, will you take upon you to say, you never were there ten times in your life?'

'No I never was!'

'Will you swear you have not been there eight times?'

'I believe I have not.'

William Davy then rapped out the question that he had been waiting to deliver.

'Were you in Edmonton before the 1st of January was twelve-month?'

'Yes, I was,' the journeyman hartshorn-scraper admitted. 'In the Christmas week.'

Scarrat said that he had spent two nights at Edmonton with Mr Hubbard, the shoemaker. When he had worked for Mr Snee, he used to water his horse at the brook next to Mrs Wells's house and had once put his horse up there. On New Year's Day, the year before, he had gone to Covent Garden in the evening to see a play. He had not visited Bedlam that night, neither had he been in Houndsditch.

Two Aldermanbury matrons appeared next. Mary Myers and Mary Woodward both confirmed Mrs Canning's account of her daughter's deplorable condition when she returned to Aldermanbury. Mrs Myers had very different views on the state of Elizabeth Canning's shift from Mrs Mayle. She agreed that it was unlikely any man had laid with her neighbour's daughter (for if she had 'there would have been nature on one side or the other'), yet she was not impressed by the cleanliness of the garment.

'Was the shift dirty?' asked Bamber Gascoyne.

'It was, but not so dirty, as if she had been hard at work in it.'

In Mrs Myers's view, the shift was just what would be expected 'if it had been worn by a person that was dragged from London to Enfield Wash.'

John Wintlebury said that he had known Mrs Canning's daughter for twelve years: he had employed her in his public house, for about eighteen months. She left him, to work for Mr Lyon, about three or four months before her troubles on New Year's Day. The girl behaved in a very sober manner and always kept in the background ('She very seldom came into our outward room amongst the customers').

Mr Wintlebury had rushed into Mrs Canning's two-roomed tenement when the news flashed round Aldermanbury Postern that Bet Canning had returned. The parlour was already crowded when he arrived, but he pushed his way to her side, as she sat by the fireside – a blood-stained handkerchief around her head – and held her hand as she told her story. He was with the crowd that jammed into the Justice Room at the Guildhall for Alderman Chitty's warrant and had ridden out with the cavalcade to Enfield Wash. Like Joseph Adamson, he saw the hay in Mother Wells's loft, the window-frame split by a great nail, the pitcher in which Bet said her water was contained. In the distance was a hill and, closer to, some trees, as she had described.

William Davy had pushed Adamson hard about his ride back to the Canning's chaise to discover whether there had been hay in the loft – and about the view from the loft window.

'Did you ever see a window in the country where there have been no hills to be seen out of it?' Davy enquired.

'Yes, I have,' replied Adamson, never at a loss for an answer, 'upon the sea coasts.'

The Aldermanbury apothecary was brought on to tell how he visited Elizabeth Canning on the day after her return to the postern. She was very weak and her face ('which used to be of a remarkable red complexion') was wan, with her arms black and livid, and her nails of a bluish cast.

The physician, Dr Eaton, said much the same: she had had 'a low, flashing pulse' and he was afraid that she would fall into a fever. The doctor had 'no reason to disbelieve her story'. As far as he was concerned, there was absolutely no doubt that she could have subsisted for a month on a few crusts and a pitcher of water.

Evening was drawing in as Morton unleashed his next stream of witnesses – to destroy the gipsy's alibi and prove Elizabeth Canning's ordeal at Enfield Wash.

The turnpike man from Tottenham road, stood to tell of the woman's voice – heard between ten and eleven o'clock – on a cold, calm night at the fore-end of January: the sobbing and the man's voice saying, 'Damn you, you bitch'. And there was the Enfield man – coming home from his shop near Mother Wells's house – between four and five on the afternoon of 29th January. He had spotted a 'poor, miserable wretch', a short-ish woman, walking very weakly. He had looked into her face and spoken to her ('Sweetheart, do you want a husband?'). It was the girl standing in court who he had seen. He had told her the way to London.

David Dyer said he saw the girl quarter of mile from Mother Wells's when he was chopping the rotten bushes. By his reckoning, that was three days before Mrs Wells and the gipsy woman were taken up. Mary Cobb – the mantua maker – swore that she too had seen the girl that evening as she was coming home from Tanners End: just as she had told the lawyer gentleman, with the smallpoxed face, who had called at her house the week after Mrs Squires's trial. The girl was creeping slowly along. She had a handkerchief pinned over her head, Mrs Cobb said, and was wearing a black petticoat with an old bed gown over it.

A vast, surging crowd was waiting outside the Old Bailey to escort Bet Canning home that night. It was noisy – and excited – but, to the surprise of one spectator, in high good humour: 'whether anything that had occurred in the court of this day's proceedings, which they might think favourable to the party they espoused, gave occasion to their behaviour, I cannot determine; but this I can assert for fact, having been an eye witness to it: that as soon as the girl had got into the house, the windows in general were thrown up; and the people, within doors, waving their hats, joined in the huzzas and exultations of those without.'

14

Wilful and Corrupt

THE OLD GIPSY was carried into court in her armchair on the
following Monday morning – accompanied by George, smart
in a red waistcoat, and Lucy and Polly – so that they might be
seen by the Enfield witnesses as they came on. First, one of Mrs
Wells's neighbours, who seemed to have seen virtually nothing
of the goings-on at Mother Wells's, and then his wife – who had
– and was convinced that she spotted the old gipsy on the
Sunday 'se'nnight' before she was taken up [21st January].
Next came young William Headland, who retold how he had
seen Mary Squires on the 9th and on 13th January at Enfield
Wash, and – what is more – had picked up the blood-stained
piece of lead from the window of Mother Wells's loft. His
mother said that there surely had been congealed blood on the
window fragment, and that her son was a good boy.

Unfortunately, William had a poor head for dates – as Mr
Justice Clive discovered, when he intervened in Mr Willies's
cross-examination – for the youth could not 'rightly say' in
which month Christmas fell, even whether 'before or after
January'. His mother seemed to be equally unfortunate; she
confessed that she had foolishly mislaid the vital blood-stained
clue that her son had picked up from Mother Wells's garden.

Then came a man who said he saw the old gipsy on the 23rd December and that he remembered the day because of a bout of St Antony's fire on the Monday or Tuesday following. And then the farmer who swore that he had seen Mary Squires on 15th December (the day he had been stamping apples). Loomworth Dane recounted how he noticed her, and the hole in her stocking, when the wind had blown up her skirt, as he was filling the barrow with gravel, at his back door, on old Christmas Day [5th January].

A day labourer – living at Turkey Street in Enfield Parish – swore that he too had seen Mary Squires, on Old Christmas Day, walking along the causeway behind his house. She was wearing a brick-coloured gown, with a red cloak and a black beaver hat. A shopkeeper, also from Turkey Street, said the old gipsy had come into her shop on New Christmas Day, to buy coffee, tea and butter, while a farmer testified that she had asked him for tobacco as he was standing at his barn door: he would guess a day or so before Old Christmas.

John Frame, Joseph and Mary Gould, Humphrey Holding and Sarah Vass all swore that they had seen the old gipsy in Enfield at various times between the 8th and 12th January, as did Anne Johnson who said she had knocked at her door to ask for victuals on the 18th January. Another woman remembered her calling at her house to ask if she sold potatoes, 'some time after Christmas', and yet another that Mary Squires knocked at her door to ask for a light for her pipe on 'either the 21st or 22nd of January was twelvemonth'. James Pratt said he saw her in Farmer Smith's cow house 'on a Thursday', as did Samuel and Elizabeth Arnot who placed the day as about eight or nine days before New Christmas.

A woman who worked for Mr Howard, opposite Mother Wells's, remembered the gipsy girl coming to her master's pump. She was positive it was the 23rd January, because it was the 'young master's birthday on the 29th' and she had made mince-pies some days before so that she could 'warm them by the fire on his birthday'.

Margaret Richardson saw the gipsy in Mrs Waterhouse's

shop in Turkey Street, and also at her own back door. She was sure it was Old Christmas Day.

'Do you know which is Old Christmas Day and which is New Christmas Day?' Mr Willies demanded.

'You must tell me,' replied the woman. 'My memory cannot be so good.'

'Which comes first?'

'Why the New Christmas Day.'

'How many days difference?'

'Some call it nine, but it may be more.'

'How old are you, good woman?' Willies persisted.

'I don't know justly,' Mrs Richardson admitted.

'What day of the week was Old Christmas Day?'

'It was of a Tuesday or a Wednesday, I can't remember which.'

'Is Christmas Day Holy Thursday or Good Friday?'

'I can't resolve no such thing; I am no scholar. I can't pretend to know such things.'

'What month is Christmas Day in?'

'I can't say that neither, because you put me to a stop.'

Mistress Richardson was not the only witness to be in trouble on her dates. Mr Willies had success in cross-examining Harriet Fensham. She was certain that she had seen the old gipsy in Trott's Walk, beside Madam Crow's garden, in Enfield – 'pretty near the highway' – on the 16th January. She was sure of the dates because there was a great snow on the 15th and she had looked in an almanack directly she had returned from Newgate, where she had been later taken to identify the gipsy woman.

'Did you look directly to the almanack?' Mr Willies cut in.

'No, Sir, not till the 16th at night.'

'Are you very well skilled in almanacks?'

'Why not,' came the confident reply. 'I can read and write a little.'

'Do you know what day of the week it is by the almanack?'

'I can; I think so. My head is good enough for that.'

'Look at this almanack', Willies snapped, 'and tell me what day of the week it is.'

Mrs Fensham took the almanack, with the sheet folded into its little book. 'I can't see by this,' she complained. 'It is so small.'

'Look at it again – and take your time,' Edward Willies reassured her.

'I cannot see without my spectacles,' Mrs Fensham grumbled as she put them on. 'You shall not fool me so.'

'Tell me the day of the week for the 14th of December.'

But poor Mrs Fensham was in difficulties. 'This is not such an almanack as I look. I look in a sheet almanack – I cannot tell by this.'

'Give it me again, if you cannot tell,' snapped Edward Willies. 'All the reason you have to fix it is that the snow fell on the day upon which you refer to your almanack – and now you have shown your skill with the almanack.'

Elizabeth Canning's counsel jumped to the rescue.

'How long was it after New Christmas?' Mr Williams encouraged. 'Was it a fortnight, or three weeks, or a month?'

'It was not much above a fortnight after,' replied Mrs Fensham taking up the almanack again.

'Do you know which is Sunday in the almanack?'

Counsel watched while the flustered dame unfolded the almanack sheet again.

'Look in the month of January,' he said.

The court waited while Hannah Fensham peered through her spectacles, slowly counting down the days – eventually pointing to a Tuesday.

Defeated, Williams called his next witness.

She lived at Ponder's End – about a mile and a half away from Enfield – and said she saw the old gipsy for three days running. First, on the Thursday before New Christmas, when Mrs Wells had asked her to call, because she was worried that she had not been well. There had been two wenches and a young man in the parlour with the gipsy. Then, on the Friday she had spotted Mary Squires in Marsh Lane and, on Saturday, standing at Mrs Wells's door. Yet Elizabeth Sherrard had difficulty in recognizing the gipsy, sitting in her armchair in the court. At first she could not find her at all, but walked up and down – looking all about her – and then went up twice to the old woman before pointing to her.

'Why this hesitation?' Mr Davy demanded.

'The gipsy was not so nasty or as dirty as she was before,' came the reply.

'Did you ever see such another woman in your life?'

'No I never did,' Elizabeth Sherrard agreed.

Then another Davy whiplash. 'What day of the month is New Christmas Day?'

'I cannot tell indeed, because I can neither write nor read.'

'What month is it in?'

'I cannot tell.'

'Was it in June or July?'

'I cannot tell.'

'Was it in June?'

'I cannot tell.'

'Was it in April?'

'No, no, it was not in April.'

'What month then?' William Davy persisted.

'It might be in June for whatever I know – I know that this is the woman, to be sure.'

The court next turned to the affairs of Mother Wells.

John Ward, the breeches-maker from Southwark, said he had known her for twenty years and – hearing she was locked up – went down to Clerkenwell Bridewell. 'Who thought of seeing you here?' she greeted him: with good reason, evidently, for Ward confessed that he had thought her dead these twelve years. The breeches-maker asked her how she came to 'keep the girl a fortnight?' It was twenty-eight days, said Mother Wells, adding – according to John Ward – '*and you know the room very well.*'

William Davy huffed and puffed at this.

'I insist upon Mrs Wells being produced to know if he knows her,' he blustered.

'That you never intend,' Elizabeth Canning's counsel remarked. And Mr Nares was right for William Davy did not pursue the matter: the last thing he wanted was for Mother Wells to face cross-examination.

A brass-founder from Shoe Lane backed up John Ward's testimony. He went with him to Clerkenwell Bridewell, he said, and heard Mother Wells say that Elizabeth Canning 'was there eight and twenty days'.

The next three witnesses that day were there for a single, clear purpose – to discredit the Natus's evidence. Nathaniel Crumphorne, cordwainer from Waltham Cross, testified that Judith Natus, talking about Elizabeth Canning at Enfield Wash, had said: 'Indeed, Mr Crumphorne, I cannot say but she really was there, when we lodged there.'

'Did she tell you they all three lodged in one room?' William Davy demanded.

'I can say nothing at all about that,' the cordwainer replied.

'There is the little word "but". Are you sure that was mentioned,' Davy continued. 'I will read it without that word: "Mr Crumphorne, I cannot say she really was there, when we lodged there."'

'She said the word "but",' Crumphorne maintained.

His wife confirmed that Judith Natus had called at their house – only two weeks earlier – to ask about a job of picking up stones. As near as she could remember, Mrs Natus had said: 'Indeed, Mr Crumphorne, she actually was there, when we lodged there.'

The reputation of the Natuses fared badly that evening. An Edmonton man swore he heard Fortune Natus lay a wager, at The Four Swans in Waltham Cross, that he was at Mother Wells's house all through January, 1753 – and had lost. A bargemaster, of Ware in Hertfordshire, said that Fortune Natus was a very dishonest man who would perjure himself for a shilling.

'Suppose he could not get a shilling by it?' Mr Davy cross-examined.

'He would try for it,' the bargemaster replied.

'Do you think he would rather swear false than truth, though he did not get a shilling by it?'

'I think he would – he hates the truth.'

'Do you know his wife?' Davy continued. 'Is she a sad wretch too?'

'She is a sad body.'

'A drunken beast?'

'You have guessed right as any man in England. You give a very good guess.'

'What,' said William Davy, feigning surprise, 'have you not made it up with him?'

'He once brought me a forged note,' the bargemaster grumbled.

Further character assassination was performed by two more Ware men. A bricklayer, gave his general opinion that Fortune Natus was a very bad character indeed; as did a farmer, it seemed, because Natus had eloped from Ware, leaving a child in the workhouse.

Then a glazier, painter and plumber, of Enfield Highway, were brought on to shake Ezra Whiffin's testimony that he had rummaged in Judith Natus's bed of hay to retrieve the iron hooks for his inn sign on the 18th January, 1753. The man who painted the sign swore that he met Whiffin on *19th January*, when he delivered it to him, and that Whiffin had told him he had just spoken to a blacksmith about making some irons to hang it on. What is more, he produced his pocket-book to prove the date, and to further swear that he met Whiffin *ten to fourteen days later*, when he told him that he had still not got the irons for the sign.

The fifth long day in the Justice Hall of the Old Bailey dragged to a close at gone seven o'clock, as Mr Marshall the cheesemonger of Aldermanbury testified – under the scullery-maid's unblinking gaze – to her unimpeachable character and perfect modesty.

*   *   *

In the morning William Davy produced a final gaggle of prosecution witnesses.

There was the knotty question of the date of the letter which had been written for Lucy Squires in Basingstoke and from which the final number of the year had been torn [i.e. 175*]. From the evidence of an officer of the Western Mail (who said that letters were only collected on Mondays, Wednesdays and Fridays), Davy showed – with the aid of an almanack – that it could only have been dispatched in 1753, for the 19th January (the date of *posting*) had not fallen on one of those days since 1749.

Then there was the testimony, to be demolished, of the Enfield woman who swore that she saw Mary Squires on the 18th January, 1753. She had dated the sighting from the fact that she took spun yarn to her employer two days before. Yet he produced a book, filled out by his daughter, which showed that the woman returned the yarn on the *23rd* and not the 16th January. He also testified to the honesty of Ezra Whiffin; and so did the High Constable of Edmonton Hundred and an attorney, who had known Whiffin when he lived in a coffee-house at Enfield. The landlord of The Four Swans at Waltham Cross also put in a good word for Fortune Natus: he was very honest, very civil and very industrious. He had never known him to tell a lie in the thirteen months he worked for him: 'I have eight servants about my house', he said, 'and I should be glad to find the fellow of him.'

Thomas Bell's praise for Fortune Natus were the last words that were given in witness at the trial of Elizabeth Canning.

Yet the proceedings ground on through the evening and into night. For three and a half hours, William Davy laboured away – making much of the evidence of the Dorset witnesses and the impossibility of anyone mistaking the old gipsy – before picking his way through the maze of evidence from Alderman-bury and Enfield Wash, examining every detail and invoking 'the finger of God' to expose Elizabeth Canning's perjury.

At sunset, the crowd packed in the streets outside had grown restive, calling death to Elizabeth Canning's detractors and destruction to Sir Crisp Gascoyne – who prudently slipped away under the protection of his friends as darkness fell. Still the lawyers ploughed on, as the bells of St Sepulchre's marked the passing quarters. The Recorder's voice failed him in his summing-up and his colleague, Mr Baron Legge, plucked the notes from his hand and read on until midnight passed.

The jury withdrew at twenty-past twelve, leaving the court to what bleak comfort it could contrive. At two o'clock a bailiff was dispatched to the jury room to know when they would agree on their verdict.

Quarter of an hour later, twelve exhausted men filed back. The foreman gave their verdict: 'Guilty of perjury, but not wilful and corrupt.'

A great shout went up. When the noise died the Recorder's hoarse voice was heard again.

'I cannot receive your verdict', he croaked, 'because it is partial. You must either find her guilty of the whole indictment, or else acquit her.'

The jury retired again. It returned within half an hour. The verdict was heard in total silence.

'Guilty of wilful and corrupt perjury; recommended to mercy.'

1 Portrait of Elizabeth Canning by William Smith, 1754

2 'A prospect of the hospitall called Bedlam for the releife and cure
of persons distracted', built 1676

3 Enfield Wash

4 Elizabeth Canning
in the house of Mother Wells at Enfield Wash

5 'Mary Squires the Gypsy, who was Condemned for Stripping
Eliz. Canning, at Endfield Wash; and has since obtained his
Majesty's most Gracious Pardon.'

6 Henry Fielding; a Hogarth engraving

7 Guild Hall

8 The Mansion House. Sir Crisp Gascoyne was its first occupant as
Lord Mayor of London

9 Sir Crisp Gascoyne

10 John Hill

11 The thrashing of Dr Hill at Ranelagh, by an enraged Irish
victim of his satire.

12 Behold the Dame, whose chiromantic Pow'r,
Foretells th'auspicious, or th'unlucky hour,
And warns the world, what wonders may befall,
To H-ll to Virtue or to Justice Hall.

13 Allan Ramsay

14 The Old Bailey, showing the open courtroom (for a healthy circulation of air against gaol fever); the front had been walled up by 1753

Justice Hall *in the Old Baily*

15 'The Conjurers', 1753
Henry Fielding (left), Sir Crisp Gascoyne (centre) and Dr Hill
(right) portrayed attempting to conjure the truth of the accusation
of Elizabeth Canning against Mary Squires from a quart bottle.
(See page 79)

16 'Jumpedo and Canning in Newgate'
or 'The Bottle and the Pitcher met', 1754

17 The Reverend
Rector-Colonel Elisha
Williams

18 House in Broad Street,
Wethersfield, built in 1692

15

The Angel of Newgate

THE TRIAL OF Elizabeth Canning was one of the most complete conflicts of evidence in English law. Never before had there been such a collision of two great masses of direct testimony, each in absolute contradiction to the other. Forty-one witnesses swore that the gipsy woman was in Dorset – or travelling from it – while twenty-seven testified, equally positively, that she had been at Mother Wells's house; nineteen gave evidence against Elizabeth Canning having been at Enfield Wash, while four swore that they actually saw her there or being dragged to it.

No detail was too small to be disputed: from the hanging of Ezra Whiffin's inn sign to Fortune Natus's morals; or the day on which Anne Johnson took the yarn to her master at Enfield Wash, and the number of fowls the gipsies ate on New Year's Day.

Dispute continued until the very end.

Two jurymen – it turned out – had been convinced of no more than that Elizabeth Canning had been mistaken as to the day on which she drank the last of the water in Mother Wells's loft. That was why the first verdict had been brought in the form that it was. When it was rejected, the two men wrongly believed that they were now committed to a guilty verdict and, in their fatigue in that final half hour in the jury room, argued only for a recommendation of mercy. Finding that they had been mistaken, they demanded re-trial. Their request was refused.

Despite the tremendous shock which the final verdict brought to her supporters, Elizabeth Canning received it with perfect calmness.

She was allowed to take companions with her into Newgate Prison to comfort her in the terrible early hours of that May morning in 1754. They were moved by her courage.

'Her behaviour was steady, serene and tranquil', one of them wrote, 'and the greatest of her concern seemed to be for her poor mother, lest she should be too much shocked at hearing the ungrateful news'.

Elizabeth Canning was still cool and composed when she stood – a tiny figure in laced bodice and ankle-length white apron – at the Bar of the Sessions House, in the Old Bailey, to receive her sentence.

'I hope', she said in a low voice, 'that your Lordships will be favourable to me. I had no intent of swearing away the gipsy's life. What has been done was only defending myself. I desire to be considered as unfortunate.'

But the Recorder was not softened.

'You shall be imprisoned in the gaol of Newgate for one month; and after the expiration of your imprisonment, you shall be transported to some of His Majesty's colonies or plantations in America for the term of seven years; and if within that term you return, and are found at large in any of His Majesty's dominion of Great Britain or Ireland, you shall suffer death as a felon without benefit of clergy.'

*   *   *

The sentencing of Elizabeth Canning unleashed a storm of paper. On every side appeared ballads and lampoons, broadsheets and pamphlets – often in several private editions, before launching into the newspapers and the *Gazetteer*.

A scholarly piece swiftly appeared in that journal, from Sallom Emylm, Esq. ('eminent Counsellor-at-Law'), giving his opinion: that as 'E.C. surrender herself voluntarily' this was a presumption of innocence; that discharged juries might well be tampered with before coming to verdict; that in an indictment for perjury it should be proved that the defendant knew it to be so at the time of swearing.

The newspapers carried an advertisement from the Lord Mayor offering a massive, £20 reward, for the discovery of anyone who had thrown dirt at or threatened the life of or otherwise insulted Sir Crisp Gascoyne and other city magistrates. This prompted angry Canningite responses that such actions were inevitable responses to the foul aspersions, barbarities and lies to which their good girl had been exposed.

Newspapers were littered with facetious correspondence – from 'Aristarchus' to 'Tacitus' and to 'T. Trueman, Esq.'; from 'Nikodemus' to 'The Printer', 'Nunckell' to 'Nikodemus' – extracting every sarcastic twist from the misfortunes of Elizabeth Canning.

'Nikodemus' – tongue clumsily in cheek – was outraged that such 'useful subjects as gipsies' should be referred to as 'vagabonds'.

> Why this is quite insupportable; surely he does not consider the vast importance bawds and gipsies are to this poor nation. Why, we should be utterly ruined and undone without them! Pray, what would become of your young nobility and gentry, if there were no bawds to procure young girls of pleasure for them?

And what was the good of 'a poor dowdy, such an ordinary creature as Bet C?' Nikodemus wondered.

> A mere drudge with an ordinary face, we have enough of such creatures; had she indeed been a beautiful damsel, with fine black eyes, and had the honour to have been a bed-

tucker to some great man, she might have found a friend able to have helped her in such time of need.

Nikodemus's oblique references to Sir Crisp Gascoyne and to the bed-tucker – Lucy Squires – was not lost on the readers of the *Gazetteer*.

Neither did George escape unscathed, in an anonymous letter dispatched to 'T. Trueman, Esq.'

> For my own part Mr Trueman, I tell you very plainly, if I should be met with, alone, by a rogue in the fields and lose my watch and a little money, I would say nothing of the matter. For how could I know, whether the fellow, who did it, might not have been formerly pimp to some great man, who might take his part, get him off, and commence a prosecution against me for wilful and corrupt perjury?

'T. Trueman, Esq.', received many useful tit-bits – all printed in the *Gazetteer*. One correspondent ['a poor man in purse and parts'] wrote, in June, to tell how he knew a man who for 'some years past he had total stop put to all discharge of nature by stool for the space of three months, during which time he both eat, drank, and walked about some'.

Not all that was published was Canningite. 'The Inspector', John Hill, was enjoying himself, even composing a ditty celebrating his own part, and Sir Crisp Gascoyne's, in the bringing down of the scullery-maid. It ended thus:

> That poor Girl young Betty Canning,
> Charged with Perjury and Trepanning,
> Now must make a long Voyagio,
> While Egyptians sing Courragio.
>
> Drink a Health to your Grand Protector,
> Not forgetting the Bright Inspector,
> Natus, Ford and Dainty Davy,
> They are the worthies that did save ye.

And there were prints and pictures galore. Portraits of Elizabeth in the loft at Enfield Wash, her bosom unrestrained or securely laced, standing at the bar of the Old Bailey; and of Mother Wells and the old gipsy astride a broomstick flying between Abbotsbury and Enfield Wash, or tramping along in her muddy old cloak. Even plans of Mother Wells's house and drawings of the loft.

There was also a poem, purportedly from the Angel of Aldermanbury herself, with hopes for royal pardon in the final verse:

> Before I fly up to the realms of bliss,
> I must acquaint His Majesty of this;
> He must take it into consideration,
> If he expects a blessing on this nation.

Not all offerings that were pouring from the presses in the summer of 1754 were from Grubb Street. Elizabeth Canning's pursuer entered the lists with *An Address to the Liverymen of London from Sir Crisp Gascoyne* etc., etc. Sir Crisp was 'not conscious of the least misrepresentation or omission of any thing' in the forty-five page justification of his action – or in the seventy-nine page edition that was later published in Dublin. He had done what he had done to prevent 'an imposture so dangerous to Society to escape unnoticed' – and the shedding of innocent blood – as well as vindicating the laws of his country. This cut no ice with the Canningites, who soon responded with a battery of publications, including: *A liveryman's reply to Sir Crisp Gascoyne's address, Shewing that gentleman's real motives, and his whole conduct concerning Canning and Squires* (three editions), *A Refutation of Sir Crisp Gascoyne's of his conduct in the cases of Elizabeth Canning and Mary Squires, A Counter-address to the Public occasioned by Sir Crisp Gascoyne's account of his own conduct relative to the cases of Elizabeth Canning and Mary Squires, A Refutation of Sir Crisp Gascoyne's Address to the Liverymen of London; by a clear state of the case of Elizabeth Canning.*

The Canningites and the Egyptians were, in fact, still squabbling – about almost anything they could find – while the enigmatic cause of all the furore sat calmly and resignedly in Newgate Gaol.

On June 1st and 2nd, paragraphs appeared in the *Whitehall Evening Post* and the *Daily Advertiser* telling of the sentencing of a Canningite witness, Elizabeth Knot, at the Old Bailey, for stealing two gowns. 'The Inspector' made merry of what could be a hanging matter: ''Tis hoped that means will be found to prove this poor injured Mrs Knot innocent of the fact, as the publick have been so well and so often assured, that none but persons of reputation and character were engaged in support of that famous and modern story teller.'

The Canningites replied that the woman had not given evidence at Elizabeth Canning's trial. She had only *offered* to do so.

Locked up in Newgate Prison, Elizabeth Canning still excited Londoners' imagination.

According to 'The Inspector' and the anti-Canningite scribblers, she was having a high old time.

> Rich is thy table, soft thy bed,
> Furnished with dainties ev'ry meal;
> Tho' once on tripes and trotters fed,
> Thy food is gosling now and veal.
>
> In their gilt chariots knights are peers,
> Into thy lap their guineas fling;
> O say, to rid thee of thy fears,
> What day does thou expect the King?

But it had come to Dr Hill's ears that a gentleman of his acquaintance ('whose office as well as character have a claim to some respect') had been denied admission to Elizabeth Canning's presence. He had not, according to Dr Hill, visited Newgate merely from idle curiosity, but with the hope that the girl would speak candidly to him.

Later, three other gentlemen (also – by strange coincidence – friends of 'The Inspector') managed to force their way into Elizabeth Canning's room. On the table were bottles, both empty and full. But worse, much worse: she was sitting with *enthusiasts*.

Enthusiasm was not to be countenanced in 1754. For Elizabeth Canning to be closeted with Methodists, and those who responded with unseemly frenzy to the ravings of Wesley and Whitefield, was blackening indeed.

On the very day that 'The Inspector's' piece appeared, handbills were on the streets certifying that the Rector of St Mary Magdalen, Old Fish Street, had visited the 'unhappy girl' in Newgate, where he had found her with every appearance of 'order, decency and sobriety'. She professed herself to be a pious member of the Church of England; the rector had been unable 'to discover any thing that could give occasion to a charge of Enthusiasm'.

Condemned, humiliated and imprisoned, Elizabeth Canning could still excite malice and sarcasm – as well as love.

> Newgate no more each rogue's disgrace,
> Sacred henceforth its cells shall be;
> Its mansion deem'd a holy place,
> Hallow'd and sanctify'd by thee.

More and more visitors came to her cell.

One intruder was particularly dangerous. Mr Justice Lediard – with Dr Hill – had helped to corner Virtue Hall and deliver her to Sir Crisp Gascoyne. He arrived at her room in Newgate professing 'great friendship' and 'great pity'. Lediard glanced at the book the girl had with her. It was *The Christians' Pattern*, by Thomas à Kempis: a surprising choice for someone whose mother said that she could 'hardly write at all'.

Did she know about Mr Whitefield, Mr Lediard asked? Elizabeth Canning said she knew nothing of the preacher. What he wanted, Lediard continued, was a full confession or, at least, that she should answer some questions. After all, there was still the possibility of pardon.

'No Sir,' came the determined reply. 'I have said the whole truth in court, and nothing but the truth: and I don't choose to answer any questions, unless it be in court again.'

*   *   *

Whatever the compulsion – pity, cruelty, curiosity or to gloat – most who came to see Elizabeth Canning in Newgate Gaol left convinced of her innocence, as Henry Fielding had been. Sheer curiosity drove William Kemp there, but within half an hour he became her passionate advocate. As did another casual visitor, Thomas Butts – who stood up to Justice Lediard when he tried to bully her – and Thomas Gibbons, D.D. (who wrote in his diary, after visiting Elizabeth Canning: 'I have reason to think that she is an innocent and injured person').

A petition to the King was prepared, signed by more than eight hundred gentlemen, merchants and traders of the City and from Enfield, recommending the girl for clemency and setting out the many circumstances that were in her favour. Again, collections were made on her behalf. Londoners were invited to leave money at Mr Goadby's, the stationer, in Sweeting's Alley near the Royal Exchange, or at Mrs Winbush's at Charing Cross. One lady alone gave £120, much to 'The Inspector's' contempt: 'We hear that the Society for the Propagation of Perjury in Foreign Parts, have collected near fifteen hundred pounds for the maintenance of Mrs Elizabeth Hathaway (a sarcastic allusion to the 'idle apprentice boy', Richard Hathaway, who in 1702, pretended to live for two months without food and 'vomited crooked pins and nails'), who is very soon to set out on her travels to America, for the improvement of her morals.'

As the time for her transportation approached with no sign of clemency, Elizabeth Canning's friends sought to pay for a cabin for her during her passage to America and for a woman to accompany her on the voyage. But permission was refused and arrangements were set in train for Elizabeth Canning to be carried on a convict ship.

The ship – aptly named *Tryal* – was lying at anchor off Blackwall, shortly to sail for Portapsico, in Maryland, with her wretched cargo. By curious chance, the bo'sun of the *Tryal*, Robert Pladger, was a friend of the footman to the Vicar of Cripplegate who promptly exerted himself on Elizabeth Canning's behalf. Would the bo'sun take the girl under his care? Pladger agreed. He would look after her. She could sleep in his cabin; he would lie outside on his sea-chest.

The trouble was that neither the crew nor the captain shared the bo'sun's noble sentiments. 'If she is put on board us, I'll board her', one seaman promised.

Captain Johns responded by discharging the bo'sun, listing his famous passenger as 'Mr Canning' – presumably to assist boarding by his crew!

News of the terrible fate, which undoubtedly awaited Elizabeth Canning aboard the *Tryal*, was relayed to Cripplegate Vicarage and, from there, to the poor girl in Newgate Gaol where the shock produced fainting fits and then fever.

The Lord Mayor was unyielding: the *Tryal* would stay at her moorings until Miss Canning recovered, when she would be taken, chained by the neck, to the ship. But he eventually relented – largely in the hope of a death-bed confession, the Canningites alleged – to the extent of sending his own physician to Newgate to examine the girl. He found her to be in genuine danger of her life. Even so, there was no sign of remorse from her and, what is more – the physician later confessed – he himself became 'more and more confirmed in the circumstantial truth of her story'.

To delay the sailing of a loaded convict ship was an expensive business and the contractor for the transportation of its cargo to the plantations appeared in court to waive his rights on Elizabeth Canning.

No sooner had the *Tryal* sailed for Maryland than Elizabeth began to recover; a recovery assisted by her friends' successful application for a warrant to take her from Newgate, while she awaited another ship. They came for her in a hackney coach at six o'clock on a fine July evening.

She sailed from Deal in August, 1754, on the *Myrtilla* – bound for Philadelphia.

16

Was Elizabeth Canning Guilty?

HENRY FIELDING SAID that Elizabeth Canning's story was like a wild dream. Yet he never wavered in his belief in it.

For Fielding, there was no mystery: a scullery-maid had been knocked on the head near Bedlam Wall, dragged ten miles to Enfield Wash – robbed of her stays – and then locked up for a month by an old gipsy woman and a bawd. And that was that.

There were snags, of course. Especially the gipsies' alibis, that they had been at Abbotsbury on New Year's Day, and the testimonies of the Natuses and Virtue Hall. But as far as Fielding was concerned this was all perjury.

Henry Fielding's immediate and uncritical acceptance of the scullery-maid's rigmarole is one of the most astonishing aspects of the Canning Affair. Especially when set against the avalanche of theories and speculations that followed. Yet Fielding's basic premise – that Elizabeth Canning was an innocent victim of kidnap – has survived, in one theory or another, well into the present century.

This too is surprising, because her testimony was flawed from the outset, in particular by the wildly inaccurate description of the place in which she said she was imprisoned. The loft at Mother Wells's was not a small, square room as she had sworn to Alderman Chitty. Neither did she mention the hay or the junk that was stored there. It was only *after* her visit to Enfield Wash – in her examinations by Henry Fielding and, later, during the Old Bailey trial – that she spoke of these things.

Canning's identification of her alleged captors was also extremely shaky. Having failed to spot either Mother Wells or George Squires, she settled on Mary Squires without seeing her face or having mentioned to Alderman Chitty that her kidnapper was so monstrous and uniquely ugly.

Yet such is the ingenuity of those who have interested themselves in the Canning Case – from the eighteenth to the present century – that these formidable contradictions have been built into theories establishing the innocence of Elizabeth Canning.

Predictably, the Canningites attempted, from the outset, to discredit the testimonies of the Dorset men. ['All the people at Abbotsbury, including even the Vicar, are Thieves, Smugglers and Plunderers of Shipwrecks'.]

Oddly the theme persisted.

Two centuries later, it resurfaced most explicitly in a study by the writer F.J. Harvey Darton. Mr Darton – a Wessex buff – was intrigued by some very curious features of the gipsy's journey from South Perrott to Enfield Wash. Why, for example, should the old vagrant and her two children appear so inexplicably in an obscure village on the Somerset-Dorset border – and steadfastly refuse any explanation of how or why they were there? Then everything becomes crystal clear – places, people and inns are remembered – before amnesia descends again between Dorchester and Coombe Bissett (obscuring a twenty-six mile overnight dash): total recall returning at Basingstoke.

And how was it, Mr Darton wondered, that the gipsies could arrive virtually penniless at Enfield Wash, and so soon have funds to live comfortably at Mother Wells's *and* pay expensive legal costs – for which there were no public subscriptions, as there were for Elizabeth Canning?

Could it be that they were agents – humble rogues no doubt – but agents, none-the-less, of the Free Trade? In short, part of the great smuggling network which supplied Georgian England with so many of its minor comforts? For Mr Darton it was significant that the gipsies had passed through Isaac Gulliver's empire at Eggardon. Such a secret organization must – according to Mr Darton – have had 'machinery' and 'capable directing brains', able to provide funds *and* false alibis.

Yet it was odd that George – if smuggler he was – should so cheerfully have shared a room with an exciseman at the inn in Abbotsbury and, on arriving at Enfield Wash, should so promptly visit his cousin, Samuel Squires – also a customs official, living at White Hart Yard in Southwark – for money to live at Mother Wells's house.

No great difficulty here either, according to the Darton hypothesis. The Squires must have been double-agents, or Government spies, playing both ends against the middle.

The upshot of these speculations is that the gipsies' alibis were 'fixed'. That virtually all of the Abbotsbury men, and other Dorset witnesses, perjured themselves at the behest of the Free Trade presumably by shifting dates to make them appear later than they really were.

Thus, at a stroke, an otherwise inexplicable conflict of evidence between the Enfield and Dorset witnesses is explained.

But the explanation is extremely unlikely – for a variety of powerful reasons. For example, by *all* accounts, George Squires was completely taken aback by the confrontation with Elizabeth Canning in Mother Wells's parlour. His reflex response was to say that he had been in Dorset ('we went there to keep our Christmas'). Furthermore, the chain of circumstances, linking each stage of the gipsies' long journey, fitted exactly and was interposed with events so singular and public – such as the skinning of the horse at Ridgeway or the crossing of the swollen Frome at Fordington – that would make it very difficult for the dates to have been shifted. What is more, there was independent documentary corroboration, notably: the exciseman's journal, giving the dates of the stay in Abbotsbury, and Lucy's letter to William Clarke – written for her at Basingstoke – which (as Mr Davy provided in court), could only have been posted on the 19th January, 1753.

Mary Squires's 'gipsy's flight' to Enfield Wash

It seems much more likely that George Squires's geographical aberrations and the funding of legal costs resulted *not* from the hypothetical support of a smuggling empire, but from the generosity of Sir Crisp Gascoyne. After all, it was Sir Crisp who employed Mr Willis of Dorchester 'to take George Squires with him in order to ascertain the places, he, his mother and sister had quartered between Abbotsbury and London'. And it is very likely that there would be variations and omissions in the ground which they re-covered. Furthermore, Sir Crisp *did* provide legal support. Including his son, Bamber Gascoyne, as a counsel at Elizabeth Canning's trial.

Thus, if anything is certain, it is that the gipsies were in Dorset when they said they were – and that their alibis were not a chain of perjured evidence.

So, total conflict of evidence remains.

Yet, even so, it may not be beyond resolution. A particularly ingenious attempt was made some forty years ago by the American writer Lillian Bueno McCue (under the pseudonym, 'Lillian de la Torre'). According to this theory Elizabeth Canning was an amnesiac; the villain was Mr Wintlebury of Aldermanbury.

That Canning might be subject to hysterical amnesia is feasible. As McCue emphasises, the hysterical personality tends to be adolescent and female; shy, emotional and incapable of pity. Hysteria can occasionally be accompanied by fits and other disturbances in physical functions, including constipation and cessation of menstruation: all characteristics exhibited by Elizabeth Canning. There is also the possibility of memory loss. And this is the basis of McCue's theory – together with the wicked John Wintlebury.

Elizabeth Canning's previous employer – the Aldermanbury publican – is incriminated for the slimmest of reasons: merely because she left his service eighteen months previously, that he owned a horse and had hurried to her help when she had returned to Aldermanbury Postern. Nevertheless, Mr Wintlebury is supposed to have arranged for his former servant to be abducted to Mother Wells's, where he later rode to have his way with her. Needless to say, like everything else that happened to her there, Elizabeth Canning does *not* remember this. Mr Wintlebury soon loses interest – hysterical amnesiacs evidently do not make rewarding sexual partners – and Elizabeth Canning eventually escapes, finding her way back to Aldermanbury Postern. Not knowing what happened to her, she makes up what she cannot remember.

The Wintlebury-amnesia theory explains how Elizabeth Canning might have been imprisoned at – and seen travelling to and from – Enfield Wash and yet could still not accurately describe her place of imprisonment. It also suggests how she mistakenly identified Mary Squires, allows the gipsies their Abbotsbury alibi and explains why she could not recognize her supposed seducer when he rushed into her mother's parlour after she had staggered home.

Yet there are insuperable difficulties. Principally because there is absolutely no evidence that poor Mr Wintlebury was Elizabeth Canning's seducer. Furthermore, her amnesia could not have been total for she remembered enough to identify the man on the Hertford coach (that she said she saw through the loft window and which enabled her to discover that she had been at Enfield Wash), also to recall that she had heard the name of 'Wells or Wills' while she had been locked up and to find her way back to Aldermanbury on a dark January night.

Then there is the awkward matter of exactly where the scullery-maid could have been accommodated with her seducer in the crowded house at Enfield Wash. Would Mr Wintlebury have been content with the loft? And whether he would or would not, how was it that at least a dozen 'inside' witnesses (including the Natuses – who would have been displaced – the Squires, Virtue Hall and Susannah Wells and her family) all denied that they had ever seen Elizabeth Canning, as did some complete outsiders: including the three tree loppers and Ezra Whiffin in search of irons for his inn sign?

It is also extremely difficult to understand why Mother Wells (who would have had to have been party to this white slavery) should have risked her neck – as also would Mary Squires, if she had known about it – just to protect Mr Wintlebury.

An alternative stratagem to posthumously preserve the innocence of the Aldermanbury scullery-maid was suggested, in 1940. Barrett Wellington, a latter day Canningite, seems to have been besotted by her. His theory is that there were *two* old gipsy women – sisters – who were so similar that they could not be easily distinguished. One of them was Mary Squires, a good-natured, inoffensive and motherly body who really was at Abbotsbury on New Year's Day; the other was a nasty piece of work, who was spending New Year, 1753, with Mother Wells.

The existence of this second, virtually identical, sister is deduced from two isolated legal incidents. The first occurred during Elizabeth Canning's trial in the cross-examination of one of the villagers from Enfield Wash. He said the old gipsy's name was Mary Squires. 'Was it not Sarah?' probed the prosecuting counsel, hoping for a slip by the witness. 'I am sure it was Mary Squires', came the reply. This was the sole basis for Mr Wellington's theory for the existence of Mary Squires's identical sister, 'Sarah'.

'Sarah's' two offspring have their origin in the names for the old gipsy's children, quoted by Virtue Hall in the confession written out by Solicitor Salt at Henry Fielding's bidding. In her confusion – tired and late at night – Virtue Hall referred to the old gipsy's children as 'John' and 'Katherine' Squires.

So – according to Mr Wellington – 'Sarah' Squires and her two hypothetical children kidnap Elizabeth Canning, cut off her stays and incarcerate her in Mother Wells's loft. Mary Squires hears about this down in Dorset (through the gipsy bush telegraph) and legs it back to Enfield Wash, with Lucy and George, to set matters to rights, while 'Sarah' slips away with 'John' and 'Katherine' – never to be seen again!

The daftness of Mr Wellington's theory is revealed not only by the origin of Mary Squires's fictional children, but also by the impossibility of even imagining that someone so monstrously disfigured by scrofula should have a twin who was identically afflicted.

Contemporary theories tended to be less baroque, as might be expected from the Age of Reason.

Like Sir Crisp Gascoyne's correspondent from Salisbury (who was 'really surprised that neither Mr *Fielding*, nor Dr *Hill* suspect that *Elizabeth Canning* might absent herself, to cover the Shame of a Lying-in'), Voltaire was of the opinion that Mlle Canning was 'une petite friponne qui était allée accoucher'. The painter, Allan Ramsay, was of similar mind, advising his noble correspondent that the case might involve 'that most humane institution, the Foundling-Hospital'.

The anonymous pamphleteer who could detect 'all imposture whatever still prevailing in the world' was firmly convinced that Elizabeth Canning had had an abortion and that it was 'no wonder she got back to her friends in such a piteous condition'.

But there is little direct evidence for – or against – the lying-in or the abortion hypotheses. Dr Dodd's and Dr Cox's professional opinions certainly do not inspire confidence. The Brownlow Street midwife is more likely to have known what she was about, but her examination took place five months *after* Elizabeth Canning disappeared. Birth stigmata would be difficult to detect after such a time. Skin pigmentation changes – for example, the coloration of the nipples or the linear nigra from pubis to navel – are characteristic of darkly pigmented individuals and would be more difficult to detect in a fresh complexioned woman; stretch marks would also be less likely to persist in a young person. So, in the absence of cervical examination with a speculum (which did not come into widespread use until the nineteenth century) it would be difficult to eliminate the possibility of a lying-in other than that *no one* mentioned an increase in Miss Canning's girth.

Another gynaecological possibility bruited by the pamphleteers was that Elizabeth Canning had been treated for syphilis. This would have involved salivation – administration of mercury by jaw-clamp – and would have produced characteristic soreness and scarring in the mouth and gums. But Dr Eaton (who examined Elizabeth Canning immediately after her return to Aldermanbury) testified that he could find no such symptoms ('Oh! Nothing like it, nothing like it, I'll assure you, nothing like it in the world: it was nothing like coming out of salivation'). In any case, blackening of the skin, such as Elizabeth Canning showed, is the opposite of what would be expected from mercury treatment.

A remaining possibility is that Elizabeth Canning simply eloped – willingly – with an unknown suitor. In the grim words of the legal historian, Lord Campbell: 'tried to hang the gipsy to conceal her own elopement with a lover'. But there is no evidence for this. By nature, she was unusually shy and modest. And there was the extremely basic, and much vaunted, absence of stains on her shift (no one seems to have ever considered the possibility of copulation *without* that garment in 1753).

Besides, it would be a cruel lover who would leave her half-starved and black in the face to stagger back to Aldermanbury. Yet this is what Arthur Machen, that strange, forgotten writer of the bizarre and the occult – whose writings helped to create the myth of the Angel of Mons who protected British soldiers in the First War – plumped for in his 1926 study of the Canning affair. The unknown lover hustled her into a coach in Bishopsgate ('whereupon Elizabeth squealed, but was not seriously annoyed') and whisked her off to a brothel. Mr Machen further conjectures that the poor girl was abandoned in the brothel the next morning, where she was left in the hands of a 'Mrs Harridan' who cut her stays and attempted to starve her into submission. She 'finally escaped at the cost of some slight violence; the famous wound in the ear having been inflicted by Mrs Harridan's finger-nails'.

Elizabeth Canning's wretched condition – especially the blackness of the face – was repeatedly and consistently described, for example, by Mrs Canning ('her face was swelled, bloated and black, and sodden as if it had lain in water, and her arms black'), by her apprentice ('she was almost dead, as black as the chimney stack, black and blue') and by the Aldermanbury apothecary ('her arms were black and livid, and her nails looked a sort of bluish cast') as well as by a neighbour ('her face, arms and hands were black; I took it to be cold or numbness occasioned by cold; her nails were as black as my bonnet and her fingers stood crooked').

Such an appearance would, indeed, be consistent with hypothermia – and lack of washing facilities. It might also be expected in the event of more direct physical violence and asphyxiation.

*　　*　　*

Despite scores of witnesses, a welter of testimony and an avalanche of writings, only three certainties emerge about Elizabeth Canning's adventures in January, 1753. First, that she disappeared – somewhere between Houndsditch and Aldermanbury – on the evening of New Year's Day. Secondly, that she was starved and brutally treated until she was black in the face. Thirdly, that Mary Squires was in Dorset at the time of Elizabeth Canning's disappearance.

All else is probability.

Now, acceptance of the gipsy's alibi necessarily implies that the evidence of the Middlesex defence witnesses was flawed. It was certainly contradictory and confused. Twenty-seven people came forward to say that they had seen Mary Squires at, or near, Enfield Wash at various times when Elizabeth Canning was supposed to have been at Mother Wells's. Of these, six gave dates that were either well *before* New Year's Day or *after* the day the Squires said they arrived at Enfield (24th January, 1753); four more guessed to within a day or so of this date, while seven were totally confused in their evidence. Thus, only a third gave anything like feasible estimates and these were remembered weeks later, with all the confusion caused by the change in the dates of Christmas, no reliable documentary evidence and the possibility of bribery by the unscrupulous John Myles.

On balance, it seems improbable that Elizabeth Canning could have been imprisoned in Mother Wells's loft. The only evidence that she *was* – apart from her own dubious testimony and Virtue Hall's perjury – was based on extremely doubtful, and disputed, hearsay: what someone thought he heard Mother Wells say in Newgate Gaol months before.

Yet three witnesses swore that the scullery-maid was at Enfield Wash: the villagers who said they saw her – in piteous condition – and spoke with her on the afternoon of 29th January.

Now the whole outcome hinges on this evidence. If it too is flawed, then there is no compelling reason to believe that Elizabeth Canning was ever at Enfield Wash. But the witnesses survived fierce cross-examination unscathed – and held to their testimonies – unlike most of those who maintained that they had seen Mary Squires at Enfield *before* 24th January.

So, again on balance, it seems that Elizabeth Canning was at, or near, Enfield Wash, in January 1753: either – and rather improbably – concealed by Mother Wells (but not in the late Mr Howit's loft) or somewhere else in the vicinity.

A priori, few obvious connections might be expected between a collection of crowded city tenements and an obscure Middlesex village, two hours ride to the north. Indeed, the Aldermanbury midwife had never even heard of Enfield Wash. Yet there were, in fact, *two* links between Aldermanbury Postern and Enfield Wash: Edward Aldridge, the silversmith, whose relative and namesake lived there, and Robert Scarrat – the journeyman hartshorn-scraper – who knew his way around those parts very well.

Of the two, Scarrat seems to be the most likely villain: as William Davy clearly tried to establish in his cross-examination of the young man during Elizabeth Canning's trial.

After all, as Scarrat so reluctantly confessed, he had lived in the neighbourhood, had known Mother Wells for nearly five years and had visited her house on several occasions since he had been in Aldermanbury. What is more, he was actually in the neighbourhood – only days before Elizabeth Canning disappeared – at New Christmas.

And it was Robert Scarrat who, when Elizabeth Canning said she recognized the Hertford coach, had brought up the name of Mother Wells ['I'll lay a guinea to a farthing, she has been at Mother Wells']. At first sight, this might seem a foolish thing to have done if Scarrat had been involved. But *not* if he knew that Canning had been somewhere else nearby. Then Mother Wells would be a useful decoy. What is more – it was said – there had been bad blood between Scarrat and Susannah Wells.

Furthermore, this extension of the 'Davy hypothesis' (that Elizabeth Canning had been *somewhere else* near Enfield Wash) would explain why the girl failed so dismally to identify her alleged prison at Mother Wells's and then fixed on Mary Squires as her captor.

Although only a scraper of stag horn (used for making ammonia for smelling salts), Scarrat was something of a Hooray Henry. He danced at Edmonton; it was said that he once rode a horse at Mother Wells's window. But Robert Scarrat claimed an alibi. After dinner on the first day of 1753, he said he went to Covent Garden with friends (a coal merchant and his wife and his landlord's daughter). The theatre was packed and they moved on to Drury Lane, but fared no better. So they retreated to the coal merchant's house. Scarrat said that he walked back to Aldermanbury Postern with his landlord's daughter. This was at about nine o'clock – half an hour *before* Elizabeth Canning left East Smithfield with her Aunt and Uncle Colley. So Scarrat's alibi is not watertight.

Now, if Robert Scarrat was the villain, as William Davy tried to prove, then there are two ways in which he could have been involved: for his immediate pleasure or to correct for past ones. It seems less probable that Scarrat took, or arranged for Elizabeth Canning to be taken, into Middlesex on that bleak January to have his way with her (the Machen hypothesis). Not the least for the fact that he was shortly to marry a Miss Carlton (his companion on the night that Elizabeth Canning disappeared). It seems more likely that he acted as a go-between, either out of kindness or because *he* had got Elizabeth Canning into trouble and wanted to clear things up before his marriage.

Elizabeth Canning's condition after her return to Aldermanbury, does not suggest that her problems were venereal or that she went to full term to produce a bastard. No one ever commented on an increase in her girth and her periods had stopped only three to five months before. So it seems more feasible that she went for an abortion which would have been difficult to detect months later.

Robert Scarrat, with his local knowledge and bawdyhouse

experience, would have been as likely as anyone to have known where such necessary ancillary services could be obtained. The ordeal of an eighteenth-century abortion explains Elizabeth Canning's emaciated appearance as well as her menstrual stoppage, both before and after the event. Her prolonged absence would have arisen from medical complications or for financial reasons. Perhaps the shillings in her purse were not enough to cover her costs. Then she might have had to stay on and work to cover her payment and even part with her stays, as Allan Ramsay suggested.

There is another odd feature which also seems not to have been considered. This concerns the evidence of the witnesses who saw her in Enfield on 29th January. Two of them were convinced that her face was pale and *not* black. One of them was chopping bushes that bitter afternoon and 'saw her face very plain'. 'She looked whitely', he testified. He did not notice a handkerchief round her head nor any injury to it. The other witness – the mantua-maker – thought the girl's face was dark but 'only in a dirty way'. Yet when Elizabeth Canning arrived at Aldermanbury Postern, every witness testified that her face and arms were black ('as the chimney') and livid and that she was wounded behind the ear.

So, the Aldermanbury maid was evidently attacked somewhere on the road to her mother's house. That she did not mention this in her testimony tends to corroborate Lillian Bueno McCue's theory that Elizabeth Canning suffered loss of memory, for there would have been no disgrace in revealing that she had been attacked *en route*; but it must have been selective memory loss, for she remembered enough to find her way back to Aldermanbury Postern and also to identify the man on the Hertford coach.

And this approaches the crux of the matter; whether Elizabeth Canning deliberately lied and, in doing so, knowingly threatened the life of an old woman, as Josephine Tey imagined in her fictional version of the Canning Case: *The Franchise Affair*. If she did, then her subsequent performance was remarkable, not only in calmly standing up to the Lord

Mayor of London and convincing most of the sceptics who streamed up to gawp at her in Newgate Gaol, but in persuading one of the greatest writers of the time of her innocence and maintaining it until her dying day.

17

Beside the Connecticut River

ELIZABETH CANNING'S PLACE of exile was as different from the crowded tenements of Aldermanbury Postern as it is possible to imagine. Set within sight of low wooded hills among lush meadows, on a bend in the Connecticut River, Wethersfield was a prosperous colonial community of sturdy, clap-boarded houses ranged along wide streets and spacious greens, with a brick-built church, *four* schools and a town hall. Wethersfield was famous for its red onions, cider making and – it was boasted – for the prettiness of its girls; Wethersfield men built schooners and sloops and Wethersfield men sailed them, as far as the West Indies, to bring back rum and coffee, lemons, limes and oranges. By odd coincidence, the river that carried them out into Long Island Sound flowed down from *Enfield* Rapids.

Elizabeth Canning lived in the house of a prominent Wethersfield citizen. The Reverend Rector-Colonel Elisha Williams, combined the military with the religious to a remarkable degree. Formerly Rector of Yale, he had fought in both French Wars: in 1744–48 as a captain with charge of scouting parties from Deerfield, where, forty years before, his father had been attacked by Indians – and had left his first wife dead in the snow. When Elizabeth Canning arrived in Wethersfield, Elisha Williams was again engaged in military duties, raising volunteers and supplies for war with the French following the news of the fall of Fort Necessity. Williams had been converted to Methodism fourteen years before by the preaching of Whitefield during his visit to the colony.

Despite her professed rejection of Methodist enthusiasm, Elizabeth Canning's supporters in England had arranged for her to live with the kindly, middle-aged minister in the tall, three-storeyed house in Broad Street, across the meadows from the Wethersfield landing. She would no longer be a servant – there were negro and Indian slaves to do the work – but one of the family: a poor persecuted girl to be cherished and helped on in life.

Elizabeth Williams had met and married her husband when he had come to England. She was a gentle, considerate woman and a good housekeeper. When she accompanied her ailing husband on his travels in 1755, she dispatched Elizabeth Canning to their property at Newington [five miles, across rolling countryside, to the southwest] leaving her husband's nephew, Ezekiel Williams, in charge at Wethersfield. She wrote to Ezekiel, bombarding him with instructions about the housekeeping, the items that should be brought from Captain Birnham's cargo – which she had heard had arrived from the Indies – and about Elizabeth Canning:

> . . . rum and whatever other things he brings, we shall want in ye family, such as sugars, coffee, indico, etc., you will save sufficient quantity. If limes, or lemons, or oranges, let their juice be saved in bottles; either with rum or covered on ye top with oil. If any letters come forth to send them hither and to lay Betty Canning's by till our return. I would also desire you to send by ye bearer ye garden seeds (I mean of flowers) which remain unsown (except those for ye borders) & some reddish [radish] seed, garden cresses, as also 2 p^d of chocolate. We should be glad of a line to know how ye servants behave, as well as concerning ye health of ye whole;

& whether Betty Canning is easy at Newington, where I wish she may continue till our return; among other reasons y^t she might become mistress of spinning. We doubt not your care of ye servants . . .

In her letter Elizabeth Williams wrote of her husband's illness and the pain which 'his sore' caused him. Shortly afterwards the Reverend Rector-Colonel Williams died, as Elizabeth Canning (who evidently had learnt to write) sadly recounted in a letter to an English well-wisher from Newington Green (who had written to say that she had invested £100 on her behalf and that, if the girl behaved well, it would be available to her on her return to England).

Hon Madam – I am so unfit to write to such a Lady as yourself as has made me offend in not writing so long, and now I do not know how to do it, but I hope you will excuse what is amiss.

I am greatly thankful for all your abundant favors to me, and hope God will reward you, tho' I can never do it, but I will pray for you and I hope that I shall never forget to do that, and I thank you for them from my heart. I thank God I have had good health ever since I came here, only once broke my leg which has been long well, only a little painful at times. I have lost my master the Colonel, who was a good friend indeed. My poor lady is greatly sorrowful: hope God will comfort her. She is very kind to me. I hope my friends will not have me from her as she is willing to keep me. I do not know where to find such another. I hope, Madam, I shall forever have cause to bless God I came to this House, and for all affliction which was the cause of it, as I always have occasion to bless God for such friends as yourself. Pray, Madam, accept my humble Duty who am your grateful servant.

ELIZ. CANNING

April 29, 1755.

Despite her quiet, wholesome life at Wethersfield and Newington, Elizabeth Canning's arrival had not passed unnoticed – even in those busy warlike times. She was the talk of the colony: even in Boston as well as along the towns of the Connecticut River.

It was rumours of a dream that caused the fuss.

A Boston merchant wrote to a friend in London about what had come to his ears.

On Wednesday Night the 30th October, Elizabeth Canning a pious Virgin, lately arrived from England (and as many here think, as does likewise several eminent sober Citizens of London, unjustly exiled), being in a sound Sleep, dreamt, that being employed at her Needle, there appeared before her, a venerable old Matron in a high crown's Hat, and antique Garb, informing her that her name was Shipton.

Mother Shipton [a reputed prophetess, of hideous aspect, who, it was claimed, foretold the death of Cardinal Wolsey] had, it turned out, told Miss Canning that she should 'imitate the Maid of Orléans' and, to assist her, gave a brief history of Joan of Arc before disclosing her vision, as recounted – in her words – by the Boston merchant.

. . . so you, my dear Babe, are destin'd to be in Revenge the Scourge of the French by the English; for which purpose, behold, I have brought you a Khevenhuller Hat with a large Cockade, a fine scarlet Coat richly trim'd, adorned with a long Shoulder-knot, and other military Equipments suitable to the present Age; as to the Sword which shall render you victorious, that must be procured from the Royal Abbey of Westminster, which, as it has before vanquished the Monsieurs, I prophesy shall in your Hands do it once more.

By the merchant's story, Elizabeth Canning was extremely gratified with her dream of Goody Shipton's prophesy. Especi-

'A Sceene of Sceenes': 'Elizabeth Canning's Dream for the
good of her native country'

ally, when she was told that it would be Mary Squires who, like
the Maid of Orléans, would be incinerated.

The account of Elizabeth Canning's improbable dream, was
followed by yet another biographical pamphlet of which there
can be no doubt as to its fictional nature (*Virtue Triumphant*, or
*Elizabeth Canning in America; being A circumstantial Narrative of her
Adventures, from her setting sail for Transportation, to the present Time;
in whose miraculous Preservation the hand of Providence is visible.
Blessed are the poor in spirit for their's is the kingdom of Heaven. Matth.
v.3. Boston printed, London reprinted*). This traces a very different
history from Elizabeth Canning's tranquil life in Wethersfield
and Newington, where the worst that befell her was her broken
leg – and that swiftly mended. According to this spoof, she
narrowly escaped shipwreck – saved by the power of her
prayers – and the attentions of a lecherous master, only to be
carried off by Indians and later, by a French friar, before
eventually marrying her lustful employer.

153

Although modest by the standards of fashionable London society, the Wethersfield social round was far above the humble world of Mr Wintlebury and Mr Lyon of which Elizabeth Canning had been such an insignificant part. In Connecticut, the scullery-maid was received by such grandees as the Treats, who had been in the colony for three generations and counted the heroic Major Treat – military chief in the 1670s – among their forebears.

Then the unlikely happened: Elizabeth Canning was courted by John Treat, greatnephew of Governor Robert Treat, generally regarded, by those that knew him, as 'a scatter-brain young fellow'. They were married from the Williams's house in Broad Street on the 24th November, 1756, but their months together were few, for on 26th March, 1757, John Treat enlisted in Captain Eliphalet Whittlesey's (Newington) Company, following news of the advance of Indians and French soldiers, up-river, earlier that year.

John Treat returned from the Indian fighting in December, 1757. But he was not with her when his son was born, because he left, with Whittlesey's Company, to advance north against the French at Ticonderoga, in June, 1758. The child, christened Joseph Canning Treat, was born a week after his father had marched away again. There was more anguish for Elizabeth, in September, when John Treat was posted as being 'dead and captivated'. But he came back from the wars, and, finally, settled down in Wethersfield with his wife and young Joseph. A second child, a daughter, Elizabeth, was born and baptised on 17th November, 1761.

The date of the birth – duly recorded in the Wethersfield registers – gives the lie to the following item which appeared in the *Annual Register* in London.

Nov. 23. Elizabeth Canning is arrived in England, and received a legacy of 500 l. left her three years ago, by an old lady of Newington-green.

There is no evidence that Elizabeth Treat ever returned to

England to claim the moneys that had been left to her.

Elizabeth lived out her life by the winding Connecticut River at Wethersfield. The following year she gave birth to a son, James, who died in childhood and then two more, John and Salmon.

She died, at the age of forty, in 1773, as was recorded by the *Connecticut Courant*:

Hartford, June 22nd. Last week died very suddenly, at Wethersfield, Mrs. Elizabeth Treat, wife of Mr. Treat, formerly the famous Elizabeth Canning.

18

From Voltaire to Video

WHY – FOR MONTHS on end – did all London go mad about a
scullery-maid and an old gipsy? And why, through two more
centuries, did they continue to fascinate? Henry Fielding, the
Lord Mayor of London, Voltaire; eminent lawyers and writers
and television people; a recent exhibition at Harvard University – all were swept up because a servant girl visited her
aunt on New Year's Day in 1753.

The conflict of evidence – the lack of a solution – are
intriguing elements. The search for justice is compelling. But
more powerful, by far, is an archetypal ingredient: the story of
an innocent girl snatched in the darkness, beside a mad house
wall, and locked away by a hideous old woman. And behind
that, again, the sinister twist that it might be Red Riding Hood
who was evil, and her awful captor who was good: as Josephine
Tey imagined in her twentieth-century version of the Canning
case, *The Franchise Affair*, which was adapted for television.

But Justice Fielding was in no doubt: Elizabeth Canning
was an innocent maid caught in the dark tide that, as
magistrate, it was his purpose to stem. More than anything, it
was the girl herself, her modesty and quietness and simplicity
of character, that convinced him. Sick – and dying in Portugal

by the time she was brought down – he reacted impulsively; as did John Hill, whose campaign of vitriol had more to do with his hatred of Henry Fielding than concern for the life of an old gipsy or the branding of Mother Wells. Both men were trapped in a web of hatred that spread in pamphlets and broadsheets through chocolate houses, by drawing-room gossip and the violence of the mob along the crowded streets of Hogarth's London.

The printed word played little part in directing the fury in the streets. The mob responded vigorously to a stark story of good and evil; of wicked gipsies, an old bawd and a poor innocent girl who defended her virginity.

Canningite hatred was directed against Sir Crisp Gascoyne, not only with sticks and stones, but by the pens of 'Niko-demus' and 'T. Trueman, Esq's' newspaper correspondents: the eighteenth-century mouthpieces of the silent majority with their menacing sarcasms about vagabonds, gipsy bed-tuckers and pimps. Even Henry Fielding was appalled by the behavi-our of Elizabeth Canning's supporters, pronouncing them in a letter to the Duke of Newcastle to be: 'a set of the most obstinate fools I ever saw. They seem to me to act rather from spleen against my Lord Mayor, than from any motive of protecting innocence'.

Religion, too, became a weapon. The Egyptians pursued Elizabeth Canning into her very prison cell to bully and foment charges of Methodism. There seemed to be a strong compulsion to extract confession – to break her – even though she had been pronounced guilty and was waiting to be transported.

Her serenity and attitude of uncrushable innocence seemed to drive 'The Inspector' nearly to distraction and Justice Lediard to push his way into Newgate Gaol to argue with her. It was as if she was inviolate. And in a sense she was, for the outward appearance of purity – whether genuine or feigned – was the final protection of the eighteenth-century woman and never so necessary as for the slavey or serving wench, trapped below stairs between male predation, her own true feelings and the hypocrisy of her own sex, waiting to trample her reputation.

And it spiced still further the public appetite for anything to do with the girl.

> Betty Canning was at least,
> With Gascoyne's help, a six months' feast.

Complete transcripts of the trial sold like hotcakes; portraits of the scullery-maid stared from shop windows; biographies and fictitious histories of her poured out. They told nothing fresh. There were no convincing conclusions about anything. It was all stale news – or rubbish! And what did it matter if it was true or not?

For Tobias Smollett such a rumpus about 'an obscure damsel of low degree' was a mystery which he could only resolve by supposing that: 'the genius of the English people is perhaps incompatible with a state of perfect tranquillity' and, if not ruffled by foreign or domestic provocations, would 'undergo temporary fermentation from the turbulent ingredients inherent in its own constitution'.

For Voltaire, the Canning case was a glorious vindication of English justice and compassion. A stark contrast with the blind prejudice and superstition of his own country, where – to his rage and shame – an innocent man could be broken on the wheel in Toulouse and made to confess to the murder of his own son to prevent him becoming a Roman Catholic. In his *Histoire d'Elizabeth Canning*, Voltaire even claimed that he had been in London at the time and wrote of the old gipsy ('Mme. Welsh') who was condemned to die, with *eight* other unfortunates, and was only saved by the decisive action of that famous Scottish *philosopher* (M. Ramsay) in persuading 'M. le Sherif' to action.

To modern eyes, Elizabeth Canning was arguably the first media product. More wholesome, admittedly, than her present-day counterparts, the whores and bawds of public men who flaunt their sins to the gutter press: the eighteenth-century mob fought for *their* maid because – they believed – she refused to yield her honour. Even so, she was a sort of pre-Saatchi creation; a nonentity – without rank or status and devoid of talent – inflated by chance circumstance, the power of the printed word and the violence of the mob. A figure to test values or release fantasies: of the stains on Red Riding Hood's underwear, imaginary adventures with American Indians or someone to fight for in the London streets. A fraud, a virgin, a slut, or the English Maid of Orléans? And to be all of these things the Aldermanbury scullery-maid had to be what she was – an enigma.

BIBLIOGRAPHY

Contemporary writings about the Canning case poured out through 1753 and 1754 in newspaper accounts (notably in the *Daily Advertiser*, *Public Advertiser*, *Whitehall Evening Post* and the *Gazeteer*), in the *Gentleman's Magazine* and in scores of broadsheets and pamphlets, most of which were listed by Lillian Bueno McCue in her annotated bibliography (*University of Colorado Studies* B, *2*(4), 223–32, 1945). Many of these were repetitive, covering and re-covering the same ground; the following were used for the present account:

Anon., *A Counter-address to the Public occasioned by Sir Crisp Gascoyne's account of his own conduct relative to the cases of Elizabeth Canning and Mary Squires*, London 1754

Anon., *A Full and Authentic Account of the Strange and Mysterious Affair Between Mary Squires, a Gypsy, and Elizabeth Canning etc.*, London 1754

Anon., *A liveryman's reply to Sir Crisp Gascoyne's address etc.*, London 1754

Anon., *A Refutation of Sir Crisp Gascoyne's Address to the Liverymen of London; by a clear state of the case of Elizabeth Canning*, London 1754

Anon., *A Refutation of Sir Crisp Gascoyne's of his conduct in the cases of Elizabeth Canning and Mary Squires*, London 1754

Anon., *Canning's Magazine or a Review of the Whole Evidence that has been hitherto offered for, or against, Elizabeth Canning, and Mary Squires*, London 1754

Anon., *Genuine and Impartial Memoirs of Elizabeth Canning*, London 1754

Anon., *The account of Canning and Squires fairly ballanc'd*, London 1753

Anon., *The Imposture Detected, or, the Mystery and Iniquity of Elizabeth*

Canning's Story, Displayed etc., London 1753

Anon., *The truth of the case of Elizabeth Canning fairly stated*, London 1753

A Clergyman (Allan Ramsay), *A Letter to the Right Honourable the Earl of —— Concerning the Affair of Elizabeth Canning*, London 1753

Cox, Daniel, *An appeal to the Public on behalf of Elizabeth Canning*, London 1753

Dodd, James Solas, *A physical account of the case of Elizabeth Canning*, London 1753

Fielding, Henry, *A Clear State of the Case of Elizabeth Canning*, London 1753

Fielding, Henry, *An impartial account of that mysterious affair of Elizabeth Canning* (an abridged version of the above), London 1753

Gascoyne, Sir Crisp, *An Inquiry Into the Cases of Canning and Squires*, Dublin 1754

Hill, Dr [John], *The Story of Elizabeth Canning Considered*, London 1753

'Philolagus', *The Inspector inspected; or Dr Hill's story of Elizabeth Canning examined*, London 1753

Information was gleaned from the following writings that were published after 1754:

Adams, Sherman W. & Stiles, H. R., *The History of Ancient Wethersfield, Volume I, History*, New Hampshire Publishing Co., Somersworth, 1974

Anon., *Extract of a letter from a merchant in Boston* [an illustrated broadsheet], London 1755

Anon., *Virtue Triumphant or Elizabeth Canning in America etc.*, 'Boston printed, London reprinted', 1757

Bacon, E. M., *The Connecticut River*, Putnam, London & New York, 1906

Borrow, George, *Celebrated Trials*, Cape, London 1928

Campbell, John, *The Lives of the Lord Chief-Justices of England*, Murray, London 1849

Caulfield, James, *Portraits, Memoirs and Characters of Remarkable Persons from the Revolution in 1688 to the End of the Reign of George II*, vol. iii, Young & Whitely, London 1820

Darton, F. J. Harvey, *Alibi Pilgrimage*, Newnes, London 1936

De la Torre, Lillian [L. B. McCue], *Elizabeth is Missing*, Joseph, London 1947

Disraeli, Isaac, *Calamities and Quarrels of Authors*, Warne, London 1881

Howell, T. B., *A Complete Collection of State Trials*, Hansard, London 1813

Kenny, Courtney, 'The Mystery of Elizabeth Canning', *Law Quarterly Review 13*, pp. 368–82, 1897

Machen, Arthur, *The Canning Wonder*, Chatto & Windus, London 1925

Paget, John, *Paradoxes and Puzzles: Historical, Judicial and Literary*, Blackwood, Edinburgh & London 1874

Phillips, Pauline L., 'Upon My Word I Am No Scholar', *Occasional Papers*, Edmonton Hundred Historical Society No. 44, 1982

Rogers, Pat, *Henry Fielding: A Biography*, Elek, London 1979

Rumbelow, Donald, *The Triple Tree: Newgate, Tyburn and Old Bailey*, Harrap, London 1982

Smart, Alastair, *The Life and Art of Allan Ramsay*, Routledge & Kegan Paul, London 1952

Smollett, Tobias G., *The History of England from the Revolution to the Death of George the Second*, vol. 3, Cadell & Davies, London 1812

Stephens, Frederic George, *Catalogue of Prints and Drawings in the British Museum*, I. *Political and Personal Satires*, vol. III, part II, 1751 to c. 1760, British Museum, London 1877

Stiles, H. R., *The History of Ancient Wethersfield, Connecticut*, vol. II, *Geneologies and Biographies*, New Hampshire Publishing Co., Somersworth 1974

Voltaire, F. M. A., 'Histoire d'Elizabeth Canning, et des Calas', in *Oeuvres complètes*, volume XXIX, 262–6, Paris, 1824

Wellington, Barrett R., *The Mystery of Elizabeth Canning*, Peck, New York 1940

Wieder, Lois M., *The Wethersfield Story*, Pequot Press, Stonington, Connecticut 1966

Willcocks, M. P., *A True-born Englishman: Being the Life of Henry Fielding*, Allen & Unwin, London 1947

INDEX

Numbers in italic refer to plates